CW01335310

How Hard Can It Be?

Clare & Jeremy Wilson

With Jane Knoop

A Story Of One Couple's Journey From Heartache To Hope

This book is dedicated to

Christabella, Bill and Pat,

whose prayers for us live on beyond these pages.

Author's note:

Some names and details have been changed to protect peoples' identities.

PROLOGUE

Clare

Mum is not alone in the coffin.

Two black and white, hazy pictures are tucked between her hands and chest. Two black and white, obscure forms caught floating in utero. They're hard to make out, as scan pictures are at seven weeks. You can see some tiny limbs and bodies with disproportionally large heads.

I need them to go with her, to lay down this dream and pick up a new one. I've lived with loss for too long. A perpetual cycle of life and death that I can't escape from. I've spent nine years trapped here; unable to disentangle myself from an invasive, uncontrollable obsession.

I'm exhausted. The hope, then loss, of these two tiny babies nearly broke me. And now to lose *her* too. I'm at the end of myself. I need a new story.

The vicar is at the front reading something about love and loss, but she's out of focus and I don't absorb what she's saying. She sounds submerged. The only thing I see with clarity is the wicker coffin.

It looks small from this angle. Adorned with a simple thistle bouquet. She loved thistles. They made her think of wild, rugged Scottish coastlines. It's why we're all in blue, not black. Auntie Margaret even dyed her hair blue. A nod to the wild thistles. A nod to her.

My senses are on mute; blurred, softened, dimmed. I don't feel like I'm in my body and it feels good. I'm still. Everything is momentarily paused. And the stillness is seeping into me; peace pervading my body. In this moment I'm cocooned, everything is held and it feels ok. I feel ok. *It will be ok.* I'm surprised by this feeling. It's a bit like hope, but it's non-specific. Unfocused hope. I want to stay here.

But then I'm back as quickly as I left. The vicar is committing Mum's body. "Ashes to ashes. Dust to dust." She's softly spoken, but it resounds, summoning me back to reality. Everything is acute and loud, hard and harsh. Even the small things feel exaggerated. My pelvic bone weighs uncomfortably on the pew. I hear Jeremy's steady, slow exhale next to me. I see the dust in the air, illuminated by a shaft of light intruding through a high window. I taste salt in my dry mouth. I smell the musty aroma of furniture polish. (It smells of death in here).

I want to put my hands over my ears and close my eyes to block it out like an overstimulated child. I'm trying to hold myself together, but in stark contrast to the stillness I felt a moment ago my body feels like it's screaming. I want to fling myself on the floor and wail. I wish we weren't so British. Right now I just want to sob.

Undignified. Unreserved. But I don't. I contain it all. I'm back in my body and it hurts.

The heavy red curtain opens and the coffin rolls away, awkwardly. It's meant to be smooth but it's jerky and cumbersome, as though she wants to go, but we don't want her to. Then the curtain closes and that's it.

She's gone.

I'm motherless. And childless. No mother, and not a mother. Caught in a space I don't want to be in.

We file out in silence. Blinking and shielding our faces as the bright April sun forces its way into our pupils. I feel Jeremy slip his arm around my waist. “Ok?” he whispers. He knows I’m not. I know I’m not. But I will be.

I still have hope. I just need to find a focus for it.

PART 1

1992–2013

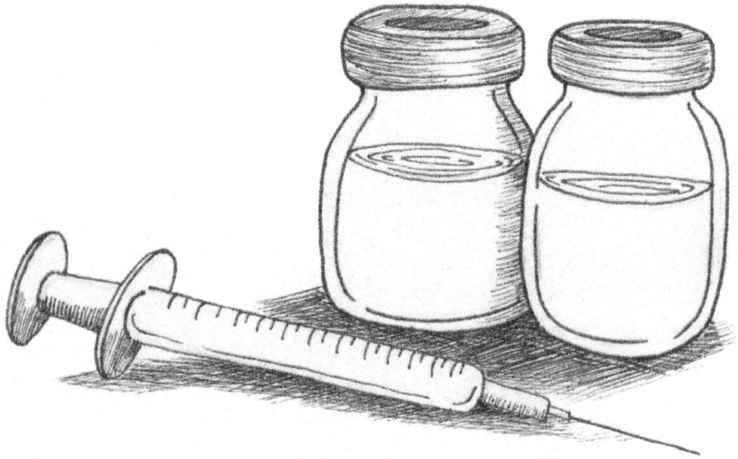

CHAPTER 1 – Sex ed

Clare

It's 1992 and I'm in a sex education class. Mrs Mellor is standing at the front with a rolling pin masquerading as a penis and a pile of condoms, probably wishing she could be swallowed into a dark hole and wondering what on earth she did to be lumped with this godawful task. This is a regular mixed state school in Petersfield, but it's just girls right now – two classes worth of sixteen- and seventeen-year-old girls – crammed together in the Home Economics room for this 'special lesson'. I don't like when it's just girls together. There's a bunch at the back, disguising their awkwardness with bravado and excessive, stifled laughter. I find it irritating, as does Mrs Mellor, who is rapidly losing control.

I'm watching her with a mixture of empathy and amusement. She's talking a lot – presumably because she's nervous – but her lesson can ultimately be summarised as: *if you have unprotected sex you will get pregnant... and you will probably get AIDS too.* The delivery is longwinded, but the message is succinct.

We get the point.

After a brief demonstration, she hands out rolling pins – one per table – and boxes of condoms, instructing that we take it in turns to have a go. I thank her as she passes me a rolling pin, briefly catching her eye. She gives a weak smile and looks away. Either she can't hold anyone's gaze right now, or she knows she doesn't need to worry about me. Because she doesn't. I meet Phil on the heath between our houses most nights after school, but it's not like that. We talk about books and history and travelling the world. It's not about love or lust or anything. At least I don't think it is.

I'm now looking out the window, holding the rolling pin and unintentionally thinking about Phil. It's an uncomfortable, accidental moment, but ultimately conclusive. It's definitely not *like that.* At least not on my part. And even if it were, we've both grown up ensconced in the Christian purity culture, where having sex before marriage is possibly the worst sin in the book and would lead to a disproportionate amount of guilt and shame. It's just not worth it.

I return to the room, passing the rolling pin to Tia. "You go first."

If possible, she's even more clueless than I am. At least I'd paid attention to Mrs Mellor's demonstration. I lean over to provide some assistance – me and Tia working the condom together – and note how this must be up there on the leaderboard of surreal moments in my life so far. And there have been a few. I seem to have a habit of getting myself into *situations;* some that turn into accidental famous friends and invitations to the BAFTAs, and others that result in me getting a half-dissected cow's eye stuck to the ceiling of the biology lab and ending up in detention.

Tia's talking but I've not been listening to her. "Clare! Earth to Clare!"

I look at her. "What?" Sheesh, her face is red.

"Your *hands*!"

I look at my hands. Significantly red-er than Tia's face. "Oh."

"Mrs Mellor!" Tia calls, pushing the box of condoms away from me like they're some form of toxic waste, and unintentionally attracting the attention of the entire class. "Clare's got a problem!" *Got a problem.* Thanks Tia.

"Oh, God *Clare*," comes Mrs Mellor's tactful response, like I chose to be allergic to latex just to make her lesson that bit more stressful. "Right. Best get yourself over to Matron and see what she can give you to calm those hands down."

I leave the classroom to the sound of ensuing laughter, congratulating myself that I've at least made *their* day.

I'm well versed in being the outsider, having moved frequently with Dad's work. I'm always the new girl. The ginger girl. The weird, Christian girl. But I've decided just to embrace it, as much as my teenage self will allow, and just be a bit weird. Or alternative. It's liberating; to be the outsider and enjoy it, not succumbing to this mad frenzy to fit some sort of bizarre, arbitrary standard. Don't we all feel like outsiders? Isn't that just part and parcel of being a teenager?

Naturally, insecurities invade my mind like uninvited parasites at times. Sometimes I feel as if something big is missing, that I'm not enough and insufficient in my own skin. I wonder if it's because I had a twin who died at birth; I should have a partner in crime and definitely shouldn't be floundering through my teenage years on my own – perhaps I overcompensate for it. But inevitable insecurities aside, I make a conscious effort not to care about the same things my friends expend an alarming amount of emotional angst on. If I'm going to channel my energies anywhere, I'd rather demote boys and make-up (lipstick aside, I like lipstick) and focus on my chosen career path. I just need to decide which it is. I keep flitting between sprinter, comedian and detective. Is there a job out there that combines all three?

"Back again, Clare?" Matron's voice breaks my career planning. "Walk into another door?" It sounds like a joke but it's not. Despite being a pretty good dancer, I'm remarkably uncoordinated in daily life. I also bruise easily, so the effects of my frequent stumbles have raised some alarm bells when we have to run through the showers naked after PE – remember this is the early 1990s. Matron has been gently but persistently asking if there is "any trouble at home." As in, does my dad hit me. An absurd thought. My dad is about as gentle as it gets. A bookshop-managing missionary who is nurturing, kind and sees the remarkable in the ordinary. But she doesn't know him, and it's taken some time to assure her that I just open doors into my own head.

I hold up my hands. "Allergic to condoms." I say, calmly, rolling my eyes and taking great delight in the expression that comes over Matron's face as she imagines nice, Christian Clare undermining her values with some boy behind the sixth form bike shed. I don't provide any further information as she raids her creams drawer for something that might help my hands.

Mrs Mellor and Matron didn't need to worry about me. But Carol... five years later my little sister Carol is sat in the same chair outside Matron's office, seventeen and heavily pregnant. Did she not get the memo that if you have unprotected sex you *will* get pregnant? Apparently not. Or perhaps Mrs Mellor has honed her message to something more nuanced now. But still. Sweet little Carol has ditched her knee length skirts and high-necked Mormon-style tops – and with it the no sex before marriage rule – opting for a more edgy, gothic look. The secret one-off with her boyfriend, James, ending up being not so secret.

Mum is remarkably calm and collected when she rings to tell me, slipping Carol's pregnancy into the conversation alongside an update on Auntie Ann and the church raffle, as if it is regular, everyday news.

I'm at my student house in Hertfordshire when the phone rings: "Ginger ninja, it's for you!" I grab the receiver, coiling the cord around my fingers, still thinking about the essay on the French Revolution I'm mid-writing (a degree in history being a fall back option, having been unable to come up with that hybrid career involving sprinting, comedy and detective work).

I am entirely unprepared for the conversation, feeling stressed and shocked as I process what Mum is saying amidst the chaos of a shared kitchen. My Greek housemates are bustling around cooking an elaborate meal while I cradle the phone in the corner, hanging on to Mum's every word and wondering how on earth Carol is going to manage the emotional turmoil. I feel distant and disconnected. Helpless.

But Mum's tone protects Carol, normalising the pregnancy that will inevitably cause a stir in our Christian circles. And as I sit perched on the kitchen worktop, listening to Mum in one ear and pans crashing in the other, I feel reassured that it will be ok. A fresh wave of appreciation for Mum and Dad consumes me; their unflustered ability to ride the waves of our mishaps with love and grace. I would later find out that the sanctimonious disapproval I'd expected from our wider community emerged in the more painful form of public censure and manipulative control (masked with a guise of love) when it came to the leadership at the church James went to. James was told he could no longer play drums in the church band and the couple were forced to announce their pregnancy to the church, bracing for the congregation's subsequent horror and alarm at their waywardness.

Hanging up the phone, I feel relieved that Carol won't have to navigate judgement from Mum and Dad. We have become so grounded in their peace and consistency. Though this wasn't always the case, which is perhaps what makes it more remarkable now. I remember Mum being angry and ill at ease with herself when we were little; as if becoming a mother was an awkward fit and she was overwhelmed with coming face to face with her own demons at the same time as coming up against the incongruous and often maddeningly unreasonable emotions of two little girls.

When you're young you don't stop to consider all the things your parents must lay down in order to make space for you. I see her in photos, pre-kids – my mum, Christabella, known to everyone as Chris – the gentle but fierce free spirit, dressed all in leather with her ginger hair escaping from under her helmet, riding her motorbike along the seafront in South Shields, going nowhere in particular.

One day, when I was seven, Mum just walked out. She packed a bag and took a bus headed out of Dundee – where home was at the time – and didn't come back for a while. I didn't know where she was going. I don't think she knew where she was going. She just needed to get away from us, from everything. But in time, as we grew older and became more reasonable, and the constant tinnitus of her past began to quieten, she drew nearer to us rather than pulling away. Reasons for escaping morphed inexplicably into reasons to stay.

She is an exceptional mum, and in this moment – as I sit and reflect on how she's delivered the pregnancy bombshell – I am reminded of how great she is, and Dad too. Two people, spacious enough to encompass their children's joys, fiascos and challenges without judgement; loving me and Carol into better humans, in the way I imagine God does. The sort of parent I plan to be one day.

Ross is born on the fourth of June 1999 at twenty-six weeks. Preeclampsia had Carol bedbound from twenty-one weeks, which is apparently very early, resulting in her feeling like a medical spectacle

– the last thing she needed after being a teenage pregnancy spectacle.

I go to visit with some flowers for Carol and teeny-tiny shoes for Ross, and glimpse motherhood in all its rawness. Carol, physically broken, emotionally delicate; relieved that Ross is going to be ok, yet still traumatised by the experience of birth. A myriad of complex emotions. Joy and anxiety coexisting.

She's sat there, her hand reaching into the incubator, gently resting on Ross, reassuring him of her steady, constant presence. I have never seen a baby so tiny, covered in tubes, being drip-fed life. There is one solitary 'congratulations' card on the windowsill. Only one person who feels this tiny life is worth celebrating. For many people in our community, the whole situation is unbearably awkward; best to ignore the fact that one of the youth group has had a baby. How people are unable to set aside their unwieldy theology and support her or, God-forbid, celebrate the event, baffles me. Maddens me. I admire her resilience and ache for her. Wishing I could somehow make it all better.

And perhaps somewhere amidst this aching, I'm aching a little for myself too. There is so much pain in this scene before me, but for some unknown reason I want to be in it. To feel the intimacy and connection of my hand resting on a tiny human who is entirely distinct and yet somehow *of* me. Surely it must be one of the most profound experiences.

When I bought the tiny shoes for Ross, I also bought some for my future child. I felt mildly embarrassed with myself for getting them, but ultimately I couldn't resist. I've tucked them away, not pining for them to be filled, and unconcerned that they are quickly gathering dust. I am simply content with the thought that one day they will have an owner.

But with boyfriends thin on the ground, or non-existent, through my mid-twenties, I have little opportunity to progress to the glorified status of *mother*. Various friends get married and start having babies, and despite the trauma of the first, Carol goes on to have another – a little girl, Beth – before Ross is out of nappies. It's exhausting to observe, yet bizarrely enticing. These new mothers seem unbearably sleep deprived, unable to do anything without time constraints and logistical headaches, and in some cases are a shadow of their former selves. But I want to join them. A mystifying phenomenon. As a teenager I was rarely enticed by the norm – actively resisting it – but increasingly I find myself wanting the same as everyone else. What is this innate draw? It's not that I'm particularly motherly by nature, and I've been far too absorbed with a PhD and a fledgling career in logistics at National Grid (detective career still pending – currently limited to gleaning tips from Inspector Morse) to give it much thought. All I know is I want it – motherhood – and one day I'll have.

Carol has dragged me to the pub. I'm sitting on a bar stool with my elbow glued to a sticky beer mat, my face resting on my hand, squishing my cheek and mouth unattractively to the side. I'm concentrating hard on not being sick. I'm aware I look pissed but I'm not – unless someone's spiked my diet coke. I'm at the tail end of a tummy bug and may have left the house a tad prematurely. Carol can be very persistent sometimes. I should have said no. I feel rough.

We're watching James' band play a set. He's rocking out on the drums to Eric Clapton's 'Layla' – as I'm informed by Carol. I'm not really into Eric Clapton. Carol is singing along and swaying from side to side with a euphoric look on her face; the freedom of a prisoner on day release. I'm guessing our mum has the kids this evening. I haven't asked.

"Want to know who's who?" Carol says, turning to me and shouting in my ear.

I shrug. "Who's that?" I say, gesturing at James. She rolls her eyes impatiently.

"So, that's Pete singing. He's the one they all made sing 'Skater Boy' – you know, the Avril Lavigne song – in front of all those teenage girls. He's such a good sport. And that's another Pete on guitar. Steve is on bass. Really nice guy. And then that's Jeremy on keys."

I nod along. I'm wondering if I need to make a mad dash to the ladies, but opt for just sitting very still instead and hoping the sick wave passes.

"You'd get on with Jeremy, actually," she adds, taking a sip of her rosé. "He's sarcastic like you... Bit older though... How old are you again?"

"Twenty-eight."

"Right, yeh. He's, like, thirty-three or something. People are trying to set him up with another single woman at church."

I look at him, stooped over his keyboard, his fingers moving enigmatically over the keys. He's looking to the right, following Pete's lead, occasionally glancing back at his music. He's tall, with short, dark hair and is automatically attractive because he's playing an instrument. He's clearly avoiding looking at the crowd in the pub, but occasionally catches the eye of one of his bandmates and smiles. He's nice. I like him.

The song ends and a few of us clap. I momentarily consider releasing a loud 'whoop whoop!', as I would have done back in the days when I went to watch my friend Vernie play on Top of the Pops, but decide it's too much effort right now. Not the whoop-whooping sort of crowd.

I'm going to ask Carol for Jeremy's number. What have I got to lose?

By the next week we're exchanging emails. It starts as chit chat. Random. Vague. He works as an associate director for a real estate company based in central London, and sends me silly pictures of himself in fancy dress on work nights out. I spout witty, sarcastic replies. And then the emails lengthen and morph into phone calls. And alongside the day-to-day banter come anecdotes from the past. He liked puppets as a kid. I find it endearing. Even more endearing when he reveals that he would run puppet shows at kids' parties as a teenager. So wholesome! He tells me about climbing trees with his sister, Rachel. I tell him about setting fire to my hair with a soldering iron. He drops in his love for renovating old buses. I tell him I'm going to be a sprinter one day, I just need to go for a debut run so my talent will be discovered. I find out that his first cassette tape was Jeff Wayne's musical version of The War of the Worlds – I have to look this up, and then tell him he should expand his repertoire and listen to Eternal. He's modest, insightful, gentle. He's funny. I'm surprised by how quickly I feel I know him, even though I've only seen him once.

Three months later we meet for dinner in a pub. It feels like meeting an old friend. Though I'm put off by how much he's looking at my chest, until I pop to the loo and realise my new deodorant is the 'shimmer' version and I've used an excessive amount, making me look like an iridescent fish. But he's not put off by my shiny fish vibes, and I'm not put off by his darting eyes.

We keep meeting, spending our weekends together, or rendezvousing halfway in London to wander around museums or go to the ballet. I even meet his parents, Bill and Pat – posh folk, but kind. Pat seems a tad suspicious of me initially – I guess she assumed her son would end up with someone in a more recognised profession. But we chat and she warms to me, and I make sure I drop in that I *nearly* finished my PhD before I quit, and that I'll probably be a detective, or a sprinter, one day.

Four months later, Jeremy proposes, back in the same pub. This time I'm less shimmery. And another six months later – following my Henry VIII banquet themed hen do – we're married in a warehouse in Watford, with a jukebox for entertainment and the meshing of our worlds on the dancefloor. I take his name, officially becoming a Wilson.

We move to Berkhamsted, near where I'd been living in Watford. A cosy semi-detached with a garden. A family home. It all happens so fast – almost a year to the day after first seeing him, stooped over his keyboard – that there're some things we've not talked about in any detail yet. Or things I've made assumptions about, seeing as our world views and outlooks on life are so similar. Like the small but significant topic of kids. So it comes as a huge relief, lying on the beach in Mexico during our honeymoon, to confirm that yes, we do both want to have a big family. Maybe four kids? Is that too ambitious?

Back from honeymoon we settle into a new rhythm of work and home-life in Berkhamsted, squeezing in a brief getaway to Paris before the end of the year. We mosey round French boutiques, sitting in cafes and indulging ourselves in Disneyland frivolities before engaging in some more highbrow tourism.

Up the Eiffel Tower I take in the view – surprisingly clean and white, even on a dull December day – and tease Jeremy that this would have been a better proposal spot. He should think of *something* to propose so this romantic moment isn't wasted. And in a dramatic ploy to stop me teasing him, he's down on one knee before I've finished my sentence. I'm now mortifyingly embarrassed – everyone is looking at us and blood is rushing to my face, even my ears. He hates attention, but he's loving this. He proposes we have a baby. "Yes, yes, of course!" I say, loudly. Anything to get him off the floor, though my answer is entirely wholehearted. I heave him by the arm back on to his feet to the applause of two American tourists, who are thrilled to have had the full experience at the top of the Eiffel Tower and are congratulating us loudly on our engagement.

Within a matter of months I'm pregnant, euphorically brandishing a pregnancy test at Jeremy as he gets off the train. He dodges the wee stick – gathering from my demeanour that it's positive – squeezing me in his arms. "How fertile am I?!" I laugh. I'm so elated it's funny. There's no sense of being lucky, just that this is *right*. As it should be. "How hard can it be?" I'd wondered aloud to Jeremy as we'd descended the lift from the Eiffel Tower, contemplating our next adventure. Pretty easy, so it turns out!

We spend the next few weeks making plans, or rather, I externally process lots of thoughts about what we need to buy and whether our baby will have ginger hair, while Jeremy nods along, equally enjoying it but refraining from getting ahead of himself. But I honestly can't help myself. I'm only ten weeks pregnant, but I've already dreamed this tiny baby into life beyond the womb.

So I'm unnerved when I notice the spotting in my pants one morning. Should that be there? The red on white is stark. Unwelcome. Maybe it's normal. It must be normal, I think, folding a bit of toilet roll into my pants and pretending the blood isn't there. I decide not to tell Jeremy – why worry him? But then I see him and immediately tell him; an uncontrollable compulsion. We agree it must be normal. Nothing to worry about. It could be any number of things, so the internet tells us. It will be ok.

But when I look again there's blood on the tissue, and then the cramps start. I go to the toilet. The horror of it. There is so much blood. Heavy clumps of it. *"Stay in."* I'm pleading. *"Stay in."* But there is so much blood it can't be ok. "It's not ok. It's not ok." I'm saying aloud, reciting the dawning realisation. *Nothing is staying in.* But still I clench against the cramping, willing my body to behave differently. I'm hunched forward, my head turned to the side, focusing on the blue and white flowers on the tiles next to me. They're all merging together. I trace the white grout with my finger. Concentrating. Up, across, down, across. I move my finger faster and faster around the edge of the tile nearest my face. A sob escapes, louder and deeper than expected. I let my body collapse into the wall, allowing the cold tiles to hold me. I'm not ok.

Through the night the cramps intensify. Brutal and relentless, as if to twist a knife and make the distress of it all even harder to cope with. I think I'm going to be sick. Jeremy brings a bowl and it waits there expectantly as I reel in pain. How did I get to twenty-nine without knowing how excruciating miscarriage can be? Why was *this* never discussed? My narrative is imploding; my understanding, my plans, my expectations evaporating. I can't catch them.

The next morning I'm lost.

CHAPTER 2 – The taboo

Jeremy

I'm trying to concentrate on the road ahead but I'm distracted by Clare. She hasn't said anything yet, but I can tell she's not ok. She stopped mid-monologue – not like Clare – and is hunched forward, releasing long, slow breaths through pursed lips. We've reached the part of the M25 where the road isn't smooth. There's a steady thud, thud, thud, as we pass over the joints in the road surface. I turn the CD player on – Coldplay – skipping a few tracks to 'Yellow'. I glance at Clare and notice she looks pale. I don't say anything. If I ask, she'll say she's fine. I'm sure she'll say something in a minute. Thud, thud, thud.

"Really. Bad. Cramps," she breathes. I reach my hand out, gently touching her back. "Not *again,*" she adds more forcefully, now bent double, clutching her stomach.

"I'll stop at the next services, though they're not until we're on the A3. Can you wait till then?"

"No, don't stop," she interrupts. "I don't want to miss visiting hours."

I contest, but she insists. I contest again – she clearly can't endure another sixty minutes in the car in this state – but she says if I stop she won't get out. Infuriatingly stubborn, even when having a miscarriage. So we carry on and I change the CD to a Norah Jones album, which seems to help a little. She sits back in the chair, adjusting the waistband on her leggings and looking out the window.

This must be Clare's fourth, no, fifth miscarriage. In all honesty I'm starting to lose count. It isn't that I'm not immersed in this, just that I'm becoming a little numb to it. Subconscious self-preservation, perhaps. If I dwell on it all for too long, unnerving sadness invades with force. It's overwhelming and disarming. An agonising heaviness that's easier to barricade and keep at bay, rather than face every day. My emotions surprise and unsettle me, creeping up on me without warning. I think it's grief, although it feels a bit dramatic to label it as that. I don't know why; any loss, of any form, hides grief somewhere in its maze, surely.

But whatever it is, this emotion feels like an imposter and makes me nervous; taking things that were once simple and manipulating them into obscure forms I don't recognise, forcing me to see the world in a different way. And even if I wanted to face it all and make sense of it, I don't even know *how* to. Where do you begin with the task of processing emotions you don't understand? Emotions you can't even name. I was so well educated, so well raised, but I'm so unprepared for these feelings. So unprepared for grief.

I know why we don't talk about it – grief – it's unsettling and uncomfortable, and we Brits don't like to be unsettled or uncomfortable. But increasingly I find it baffling that we avoid such a universal experience, each of us left to flounder on our own; ill-equipped and isolated. Even in church, we're good at being jubilant, and less good at sitting with our lament and sorrow, despite it making up such a significant part of life.

It's been well over a year now of regular pregnancies and miscarriages. I was alarmed initially, woefully unaware of the statistics; one in four pregnancies end in miscarriage, apparently. It's not as uncommon as I'd thought. Not that I'd ever really thought about it; I'd never had reason to. I knew miscarriage was a thing, but had never needed to give it any headspace. It's not the sort of thing that comes up in conversation, at the pub, around the dinner table, or by the coffee machine at work. It would make for awkward conversation, so we don't mention it, opting for silence. Shutting off the emotion and feeding the taboo.

The first miscarriage was the hardest. Clare was in intense physical pain. I wanted to share it with her. I wanted to take it from her and feel it for her, but I couldn't. I could only watch and wait, cry and console.

Now I wonder how many friends and acquaintances of mine have been through nights like the ones Clare and I have been through this past year – acute pain for Clare and crushing disappointment for us both – and then rocked up at work the next morning, cracking on with the next task as if nothing remotely traumatic has taken place. It makes sense. It's what I've been doing too; finding it infinitely easier and more productive to press on, enveloped in life's daily distractions. Talking about it makes it all too real, magnifying the dismay and opening up emotional – and physical – floodgates I've been indirectly taught to keep shut.

But somehow, amidst the mess of emotions, we still have hope. Picking ourselves up and carrying on isn't just an evasion tactic; hope is real, genuine and motivating. We're still hopeful that one day, we'll have a child. Hopeful that *this* pregnancy will be the one. This steady supply of hope sustains us, giving us energy. And this hope-fuelled energy seems to seep into the rest of life, enabling us to look beyond the sadness and have fun, genuinely enjoying life; seeing friends, going to gigs, travelling to far flung destinations on our bucket lists (Jamaica's next). So with the disappointment of each miscarriage there are also multiple reasons to carry on, cautiously optimistic that this won't be our story forever. Three in four pregnancies result in a child. One of Clare's pregnancies surely will.

Clare keeps leaning across to check the clock on the dashboard. Visiting hours are between two and seven. M25 traffic has slowed us down – why did we decide to travel in rush hour again? We're cutting it fine, and Clare wants as long as possible with her mum. I speed up a tad. Thud, thud, thud.

Chris was diagnosed with breast cancer last month. Clare's nana, Chris' mum, also had breast cancer, so Chris has had regular precautionary scans. But somehow they missed it. So they've decided to go straight for a double mastectomy, followed by chemotherapy and radiotherapy treatment, to make sure they 'get it all'. It's hard to gauge how serious it is. It seems serious.

Clare's close to her mum, increasingly so. Since experiencing baby loss she's discovered that her mum also had miscarriages, and that conceiving Carol was nothing short of a miracle. I appreciate why you wouldn't share your most painful experiences with your children, especially when they are in the past, but finding this out surprised Clare – and me – reminding us both of how little we know about the lives our parents lived before us. Clare always knew she had a twin who died, and Chris was apparently very candid with Clare and Carol growing up, explaining the female anatomy and mechanics of sex in excruciating detail for teenage ears. But she never mentioned miscarriage. Again, the unspoken taboo.

"We're going to have to stop," Clare says abruptly, gesturing at the sign for motorway services and fishing a sanitary pad out of her bag. When we eventually reach the services, she's out of the car before I've turned the engine off, making a mad dash across the car park for the toilets. I wait, watching the rain hit the windscreen. Pathetic fallacy reminding me that however hopeful we are, in the moment it can feel pretty bleak.

I find Clare remarkable. Stoically coping with the emotional and physical toll of miscarriage. This has become our norm, but it shouldn't be, and I can see how devastating it is for Clare. Slowly chipping away at her. It's our burden, but it weighs most heavily on her. I feel a responsibility to be positive and upbeat for her sake. It's not as real to me on a day-to-day basis; I don't have to navigate the hormones, the physical pain and the bleeding. Last year she jokingly asked me for a baby for her birthday. It was light-hearted; "I'd like a rubber duck and a baby please! And a chocolate cake shaped like a handbag." But it also wasn't light-hearted, it was serious. She really did want a rubber duck (a weird Clare-obsession) and she *really* wanted a baby. But another year's gone by and it's not happened. I'm almost tempted to ask for a baby for my birthday too; the desire for a family is escalating, verging on desperate, but totally out of our control.

On Sunday, while I was helping pack away equipment after the morning service at church, I noticed Clare meeting our friends' new baby. They had a miscarriage last year – so I'm told by Clare – and now here they were, cradling their child. More hope for us, and yet more aching in the moment. I surreptitiously watched Clare smiling and cooing; graciously holding this baby when plopped unquestioningly in her arms. She was unusually quiet on the way home, expressing her genuine pleasure for our friends, sharing in their delight and celebration, and musing on how great it was that they'd been able to have a baby after having had a miscarriage. And then she trailed into silence, unable to find the words to say the second part of what she was feeling, which would probably have sounded something like: *but it also makes me so sad and envious and confused.* The confusion is real; believing in a loving God who delights in giving good gifts to his children, but who seems unable to delight in gifting *us*. We hold on to the reality that we're equally loved – we don't believe in an arbitrary God – but it's hard, and confusing when your lived experience doesn't mesh neatly with your theology.

Back on the road, I notice that Clare is silently crying. Wiping tears and snot on the sleeve of her jumper. As if on cue, Norah Jones' 'Come away with me' comes on. It was playing in the pub when I proposed, and it was the song for our first dance at our wedding. I'm worried it's going to make her cry more, despite the fact that it evokes happy memories. Sentimental things often make her cry, regardless of the emotion attached. I'm wondering whether I should change the CD to something more upbeat – Kylie Minogue, or Eternal, if I can bear it. Clare and I have very different tastes in music. But she's singing along now, so I think we're safe. And in the absence of words – anything would fall short right now – I reach across and take her hand.

We're nearly at the hospital. It feels a bit odd to be approaching the facility with a wife having a miscarriage, but not to be coming for her sake. Initially Clare sought medical support, going to the GP a few days after her first miscarriage. In their tired, burnt-out state the GP was unable to dig deep enough to emotionally engage, opting rather to berate Clare for not having gone straight to the hospital. So with her second miscarriage we did go straight to A&E, which turned out to be an equally clinical, insensitive experience with her being 'cleaned out' and then told to take another pregnancy test just to 'check that there's nothing there.' I appreciate they needed to get a job done, but it resulted in Clare choosing to manage her subsequent miscarriages at home. She tends to just go to her mum, a former midwife, or Carol, who's training to be a nurse, if she needs advice. On occasions she's reached out to her cousin who is a fertility doctor, although it doesn't seem that our struggles are fertility related. Clare *can* get pregnant, relatively easily it seems. She's just unable to carry a baby past ten weeks. I'm beginning to wonder whether it would be worth getting some tests done to find out what the problem is.

We park up and feed all our loose change to a hungry ticket machine before heading inside. Up in the cancer ward we find Clare's dad, Mike, waiting by reception. Chris is sleeping, so he's decided to wait before going in to see her. Clare gives him a quick hug and heads straight for the loos.

Hospitals don't feel like the right place for inane chit chat, so I hesitate, unsure of what to talk to Mike about once we've covered the obvious topic of Chris and the operation. But Mike is upbeat – unrealistically so – and seems to want to chat. I wonder if he's summoning extra positive energy for Clare's sake. Or maybe he's motivated by the hope that the last-resort-mastectomy will lead to Chris being cancer free.

"Work going ok?" he asks in his disconcertingly jolly tone.

"Oh yes," I say. "You know, the inevitable personality clashes to navigate, but generally good." I decide it's not the right time to tell him I'm thinking about leaving. I've been working for this particular real estate company for nearly ten years and I'm ready for a change. There was an unfortunate moment on a business trip in Frankfurt last month when we were having dinner. I don't recall us having had a huge amount to drink, but my boss went to the loo and came back and sat at the wrong table. When he realised his mistake and rejoined us, I made a genial joke about it – the sort of thing he would have said to me. It didn't go down well. I sense I'm being ostracised now, which I've ultimately got no qualms about. It's well timed, coinciding with an opportunity to work with some consultants, and I'm even considering a part-time job as information systems manager for a charity linked to our church.

Another pause, as I ponder how much of this to share with Mike, during which Clare appears, tripping on a 'Caution: Wet floor' sign. She's clearly a bit zoned out.

"Ok?" I ask. I'm concerned and I know it shows, as she gives me a weak, reassuring smile. She turns to her dad and I decide to give them a moment and head for the coffee machine.

I'm sure I put the code in correctly but the stupid thing is spitting out milk into the little beige plastic cup. I try again, hitting the code for black coffee hard with my thumb. I'm usually pretty unflappable, but there's a bit too much going on right now – around and within. I'm trying to be composed but I'm feeling increasingly stressed.

"I'm so sorry," Mike says as I rejoin them. Clare must have told him about the miscarriage. He's a really kind man, empathy comes naturally to him. But I don't know what to do with his concern right now, so I just tell him it's ok, when it's not.

"Milky coffee?" I offer him my first attempt at coffee and he accepts it. I can't remember if he actually likes coffee or not, but either way he seems pleased to have something to hold. Something to do. I steer Clare towards some chairs before she keels over.

"Maybe you should ask for some help?" I suggest. "We are in hospital after all. We could pop down to A&E after we've seen your mum?"

"No, it's fine. I'll be ok." I nod, unconvinced, getting her a cup of water from the cooler in the waiting room.

"Anything else I can get you?"

She shakes her head, rummaging in her coat pockets. "I need to message Carol," she retrieves her phone, various old tissues and wrappers spewing out at the same time. I pick them up. "About Mum, not the baby," she adds. "She wants regular updates." There's a pause. "I'm not going to tell Mum about losing this baby either, by the way." She doesn't look up from her phone. "I don't want to upset her when she needs to recover." I nod again, but doubt if she'll be able to follow through with this when they're face to face.

Mike comes over, plonking himself down next to us and I quickly grab a newspaper from the table on the other side of Clare. Whilst most people don't want to talk about miscarriage, Mike is the sort of person who might ask me some sensitive questions, and I don't want to talk about it right now. Or anything else really. My social tank is low. I lick my fingers and tease apart the pages of the newspaper.

A short article on the second page tells me that a two-year-old boy was killed in a house fire in Brixton. I flick over. 'Tax cuts are essential to beat crisis says minister'. I flick again. 'First view of private photos of the Queen on holiday'. I flick again, but I'm thinking of the two-year-old who was killed. I'm thinking of his parents. The unimaginable grief of losing a child.

I feel like we know what it's like, but at the same time tell myself that we don't, of course we don't. We never met our babies. They were only ever a dream. We never *held* them or kissed them. Imagine burying a child you've embraced, loved, *known*. That must be infinitely worse. Perspective, I tell myself. Get some perspective. But as I momentarily berate myself, I know this isn't what I'd be saying to someone else in my situation. I would be validating their loss, not belittling it.

A nurse comes over. Chris is awake now. We rapidly grab our coats and coffees. I loiter behind as Mike and Clare go in, settling themselves in chairs as close to the bed as possible, leaning forward to kiss her on the forehead. It's a busy ward so I draw the curtains fully round us.

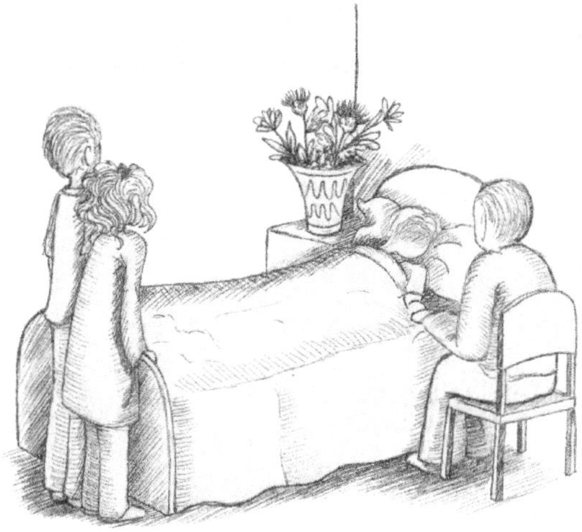

She's recovering from a major operation but still finds the strength to greet me and ask me how I am. "Fine thanks, Chris. Fine." It feels strange to be asked how I am when absolutely none of this is about me. She's generous, even when on a recovery ward. I look at Clare and see that she's struggling to hold it together. After about ten minutes of Mike rearranging pillows, and Chris summoning all her energy to show Clare how well she's doing, Clare cracks.

I look at Mike and we both slip out a gap in the curtain, leaving the two of them to share their respective pains, and grieve together.

It's gone eight-thirty by the time we get home. I'm exhausted as we pull into the drive. I can't imagine how Clare's feeling. My cat, Borric, is waiting by the front door guarding a suspicious looking white box in the porch and living up to his namesake – Lord Borric from Raymond E. Feist's fantasy novel, *Magician*, who fearlessly protects his kingdom.

I scoop him up, scratching him behind the ears. "What a fabulous guard-cat," I coo, aware I'm using my slightly higher, slightly sweeter 'cat voice'. I think it's akin to the voice other people use when talking to babies or small children.

"Ah, the cake!" Clare exclaims from behind me, spotting the white box.

"Cake?" I'm confused. We're expecting cake?

"Yes, you know!" I don't, but I don't say anything, waiting for her to elaborate, which she will. "For your dad's retirement party tomorrow?"

That's tomorrow? Gosh, it's been a long week, and apparently I'd forgotten that we're driving up to Granny's in Stevenage tomorrow.

"You asked for me to do him a gardening cake? Well, I ordered one," she reminds me as we head inside. She pops the box on the kitchen worktop and opens the lid. "Oh."

I join her and we stand and bear witness to the most ridiculous cake I've ever seen. It's round, covered in pink, frosted icing, which I think is meant to be a skirt, and protruding from the middle is the bottom half of a Barbie, complete with pink garters and frilly white pants.

"Oh indeed..." I'm searching for something to say to try and minimise the disappointment. Clare doesn't need any more disappointment today. "He'll love it," I add. He won't, most definitely *won't*. He wouldn't even find it funny. He loves a joke, but not this kind. He's far too proper for this sort of frivolity.

Clare shuts the box. "I'll fix it in the morning." Pause. "It will feel better in the morning."

I know she's not talking about the cake anymore.

CHAPTER 3 – Hormonal mess

Clare

"You're back!" Frank mouths from the other side of the glass wall. The photocopier is so loud I can't hear him, but context and my honed lip-reading skills would suggest that's what he's saying. I give a manic smile and wave both my hands. I don't know why I'm doing the jazz-hands thing. It's weird. Maybe I'm overcompensating for the post-holiday blues.

"Still waiting for those to go brown then?" Frank says as he comes in, winking and gesturing at my pink arms. I laugh. Usually I pride myself on my quick, witty responses to banter – I work in a very male environment so have plenty of practice – but I'm too tired to think today. Yes, I got very burnt on the last day in Jamacia. And no, I'm not *waiting* for the burn to turn brown. I never go brown.

"Good holiday?" he adds, gleaning from my glazed expression that this is not the moment for banter.

"Yeh, amazing thanks." I'm wondering how to summarise the last few weeks. Now that I'm back to normality, care-free Clare hanging out with a mocktail watching a Jamaican sunset doesn't feel real. "We went to see Bob Marley's tomb." I add. A bit random. I'm not sure why I've shared this fact, but I guess it was one of the more memorable moments from our holiday, not least because I somehow managed to set fire to my skirt on the candles lining the inside of the tomb.

Frank starts singing 'Three Little Birds'. I join in but feel annoyed as I definitely don't feel that 'every little thing is gonna be alright' this morning. When we were away we were living in the moment; I was lost in it, not longing or angsting or hoping or despairing. Just being, and enjoying life. Everything *did* feel like it was gonna be alright. But this morning, reality has wormed its way into my mind and attitude, reminding me of the underlying sadness shrouding my life.

I woke up to the news that another friend is pregnant. Twelve weeks. She's had a scan and everything. I'm exhausted by the fact that I don't just feel one thing in response to this. I feel extremes. I'm genuinely happy. Genuinely thrilled. I'm also anxious – pregnancy isn't straightforward, I really hope it goes ok for her. And I'm a whole mess of other emotions I can't identify. I'm heavy. I'm numb. I'm throbbing somewhere internally. I'm desperate for this to be me, sharing my scan, revealing to the world our wonderful news. But it's never me. I'm eight weeks pregnant right now, but I'm not allowing myself to think about it. I'm shutting this one out, too tired to hope. Bored by my own anxiety and envy. Tired by feeling so out of control.

I'm also worried about losing another friend. It sounds extreme, but it's just how it goes. They have a baby and move into another sphere of life; making new friends on maternity leave, no longer available in the evenings, going to baby groups, switching to the family service at church. Naturally, they can't remember a time before they became a mum. It's all-consuming. I see that. I want it. But I end up being the one left behind, the one who can't fully identify; the honorary aunty, the godmother, the available, childless friend.

"Wish I could just leave the kids and go sun myself in Jamaica for a few weeks! You should enjoy the freedom while you have it, it must be great!" Frank says, pausing from his singing, unaware of how insensitive this comment is. However great Jamacia was, I'd choose a family over a holiday in a heartbeat. "How long you going to be with that?" he adds, gesturing at the photocopier.

Crap. I've not been paying attention. How long has this thing been going? And why are there so many copies of *Company Merger Agenda* spewing onto the tray? I look at the little screen. 93 of 100 copies. 94 of 100 copies. I hit the stop button, gathering up the unintentionally large pile. "All yours!" I say to Frank, dumping the eighty-four copies of *Company Merger Agenda* I *don't* need in the scrap paper tray on my way out the door.

Despite my demeanor I'm glad to be back at work. Last year, National Grid was bought by an umbrella company; I reapplied and got the role of information manager, which started out as reporting but has become more eclectic. I find work diverse and absorbing. Generally people don't talk about babies and children, and I don't think about miscarriages or the fact that I'm pregnant. Sometimes my body reminds me; exhaustion, sore breasts, weight gain. But my hormones have been in such disarray these past few years that I've become accustomed to it. I'm forgetting what's normal and what's not.

On the way back to my desk, dodging a few more 'where's your tan Clare?!' jokes, I get *that* sensation. The trickle. I'm hoping I've just wet myself. Which is a weird thing to hope for – loss of bladder control at 32. I about-turn and head for the loos. Only to discover it's not wee. It's blood. I'm on autopilot, tucking some tissue in my pants and heading back to my desk, a few cheery 'hellos!' on my way. I locate my pads. Maternity pads. They're obscenely large, like wearing a nappy. I tuck one up my jumper and head back to the loos, laughing at the 'incontinent already Clare?!' not-so-funny-joke on the way. Thankfully there's no queue. There's never a queue, I'm one of only two women in the office. But I'm still thankful. And I sit there for a while in the silence. It hurts, but I don't think about it. I just sit there. Not thinking. Not feeling. Just sitting.

After a while my mind wanders to the pregnancy test I took last month. What if I could pretend I'd never taken it? Forget that I'd ever seen those two hopeful lines on the stick? Then this would just be a really (really) late period. Granted, an excruciatingly painful one, but just a period. Not loss, not grief. Just menstruating, as nearly every post-adolescent, pre-menopausal female does.

I glance at my watch. Meeting in five. I pop the pad in, splash my face with cold water and head off to tell my colleagues how refreshed I feel after my holiday and attempt to contribute something to the discussion about our next company merger.

I'm meant to be meeting Jeremy for dinner after work – Golden Dragon Chinese restaurant just off Leicester Square, the dumplings are heavenly – but I'm not sure I feel up to it. I pause at the station, wondering which way to go – north, home, or south, dumplings. The draw of the Golden Dragon is too strong. I grab an Evening Standard and head southbound towards Leicester Square.

Over dinner I casually mention to Jeremy about the potential baby no longer being potential as I slurp up my noodles, and then go on to tell him about the ins and outs of the latest company merger. He doesn't care about the company merger. He cares about me. And he thinks we should go and see a GP and get to the bottom of things.

"How many is this now, Clare?" He asks, putting down his glass and reaching across the table to steady my hand. I hadn't noticed it was shaking.

"Eleven." I take a breath, finally feeling submerged in the distress I've held at bay all day. "We've lost eleven."

I want to ignore the distress. But sadness is constantly stalking me, tracking me down and holding me captive. I can feel it creeping closer. I busy myself with adding more soy sauce. Avoiding Jeremy's eye contact. If I catch it I'll cry.

I want to forget. I want to forget about each tiny life that's grown inside me; each foetus that shook our world and changed our plans. The tiny lives I've been so eager to name, impatient to know, desperate to love. I want to forget about them.

I tell myself that it's not so bad, it could be worse. Life could be worse. I'm so lucky. There is so much to be grateful for. But I still feel *so* sad. I can't help it. And I don't know what to do with it or where to put it. I can't sit with my sadness, I can't bear it. But I can't bury it. So what do I do? Just drag it around as an uncomfortable load and wait for it to catch on something and fall away.

Right now sadness has caught. But it's not fallen away, it's suffocating me. I look at Jeremy, hold his gaze, and sob silently into my noodles.

The GP told me off for not coming sooner. Fair. I probably should have. But I was encouraged by his concern and pleased that he referred us to a consultant at a well-regarded clinic in St Albans. Once there, we discovered that the other doctors in this clinic seem to operate in fear of the consultant. Does that bode well? Is he scary because he's intimidatingly good at what he does, or just an asshole? The jury's out. We didn't see him when we were there, he remained this ominous figure. The doctors would occasionally scurry out and ask him something and scurry back in, relaying his advice. He advised we had various fertility tests done, which I couldn't help but feel was a bit off beat. Did he hear that we *can* get pregnant? That our trouble is more with being unable to retain the pregnancy? I assume he did – this is a well-regarded clinic after all.

So we roll with the advice and get the tests done, but the results are inconclusive; they can't find anything wrong with us. We *should* be able to have a baby. I don't know if I feel encouraged by this or not. They decide to offer us three rounds of IVF – In Vitro Fertilisation – on the NHS. I'm not sure why this would be any more successful than getting pregnant naturally, but maybe there's something about IVF that would mean the baby stays put. We're hopeful. Really hopeful. It's refreshing and energising.

And we feel even more hopeful when we start searching around for clinics. So many stories of success with IVF. Another clinic, another brochure or website with pictures of parents gazing at newborns. Occasionally we'd read a story of a failed round of IVF, usually with some subtle justification – too much stress in the client's life – but then the next round would result in their longed-for child. 'This is your year to become a family', one clinic told us. And I'm beginning to believe it. I'm savvy enough to be aware that sometimes IVF doesn't work, but surrounded by this propaganda infiltrating my optimistic tendencies, I'm feeling pretty confident that this is our year.

Two of my friends are also just starting out on IVF, so we've decided to form a support group. They're both very Christian. I'm not entirely sure what I mean by this, as I know one Christian is not more Christian than another – all equal, all one in God's eyes – but there's something a bit more 'holy' about them. I'm pretty sure they wouldn't swear or doubt; I swear a bit and doubt a lot these days. I'm wondering if their prayers will carry me. I feel the need to ride the waves of other people's belief right now.

I grew up in Christian communities where miracles were second nature. I saw things, *experienced* things I find hard to deny. There was so much faith, it was contagious. There are pictures of me sitting on the famous evangelist Billy Graham's knee as a toddler, absorbing the electric atmosphere. God interacting with daily life was expected and normal. It was part of my identity.

For the first eight years of my life I relied entirely on lip reading and sign language, having been born deaf, until I was prayed for and suddenly found I was able to hear. This sort of miraculous experience was my reality. So how do I make sense of that now, when God feels elusive and distant? I still sense him, but it's subtle – he's in a friend's intuitive kindness or the majestic oak tree. I see him in the daily things, a reassurance that he's present, *with* me. But I don't see him in the big stuff.

I have been told – a lot – that if I pray with faith, God will hear and respond. I have been told – a lot – that if I delight in God, he will give me the desires of my heart. So I summon my faith and delight and pray for a child. Do I not have enough? Is my faith inadequate? My delight insufficient? I'm even beginning to wonder if I've done something wrong, having strange urges to dig back through my catalogue of wrongs and re-confess anything I can, just in case there is something standing in the way of me and an answered prayer. I know God doesn't work like this, he doesn't require me to crawl on my knees, grovelling. He's a loving father. He delights in me. I *know* this, but if I'm honest, I don't feel it. Sometimes I wonder if I still believe. But the wondering is momentary; for some reason I can't *not* believe. I'm compelled. This is my heritage. My mother-tongue. And I'm still captivated by God, despite my confusion. Maybe this is just faith at its rawest.

We've picked our clinic. It has a good success rate, and it's equidistant from home and my office and adjacent to the canal, giving it an air of tranquillity. I'm feeling extremely positive as we arrive. Jeremy too. Our sarcastic banter has been on overdrive this morning but it's very quiet in the waiting room, almost spa-like with plinky-plonky music and a fish tank, so we pipe down and wait in silence, looking at the pictures of babies on the wall. 'Dreams do come true', we're told explicitly by a brochure on the coffee table.

I feel unexpectedly nervous when we're called in. Maybe it's anticipation. It's hard to tell. There is a clear 'Pull' sign on the door but I frantically push until Jeremy whispers, "try pulling it, Clare" in my ear. I open the door with force into my head. "My wife, ladies and gentlemen," Jeremy mutters. I give him a thump.

We see the nurse first, who's not quite sure what to make of us from our entrance and seems more concerned about my head injury than anything else, repeatedly asking if I'm ok as she takes us through filling out some consent forms. I feel a bit dizzy when she takes blood for a screening test – I'm really hard to get blood from and it takes three attempts – but I don't mention anything and let Jeremy do all the door opening as we go through to see the consultant. Jeremy looks chivalrous and I look less like a dingus – it's a better first impression.

The consultant, Paul, has all our notes from our referral but we still have to go over everything in detail again so he can assess whether we need the treatment. Despite his warm, professional demeanour, I feel anxious. This is a strange sort of test. What if he disagrees with our referral? But he doesn't. Eleven miscarriages seems sufficient for him. He says something about how awful it must have been and how he's here to help. I'm so reassured I could cry.

"One of the most important things is that we make sure you're both physically and mentally ready for the process," Paul says, looking away from his screen and removing his glasses. "I see your BMI is a bit high, Clare." I'd made a point of not looking at the little arrow when the nurse weighed me. I know I've put on weight, but I don't really want to know how much. I've embraced the weight gain as part of the frequent pregnancies. My body's been through a lot, and I feel this unexpected connection to my weight, as if it represents the babies my body has held. I feel a strange resistance to losing the weight I've gained over the last few years. My 'baby weight'. But here's my motivation: I need to get down to twelve stone in order to go ahead with IVF. I need to shake two stone and I'm raring to go.

As soon as we're home my bike comes out the shed. Jeremy gives it some TLC and I start cycling everywhere. I'm a bit nervous on roads, aware of my tendency to swerve, and Jeremy seems constantly relieved when I come home alive. But the bike – which I've become fond of and called Mabel – combined with a liquid diet is effective and I'm seeing some satisfying results in a matter of weeks. I wouldn't be able to do this without serious motivation and I'm not sure if anything else could be more motivational than this: the prospect of a baby. It's tantalising.

A few weeks later we're back at the clinic for our treatment information appointment. We've done our research, but despite this Paul goes through the whole process in detail, making sure we're aware of what lies ahead. I'm listening intently but start wondering whether I should be taking notes, as I can't remember everything he's saying, which then makes me wonder where my notebook is and whether it might actually be in the car and whether I should pop out and fetch it. By the time I've decided I can't be bothered to pop back to the car and have tuned back into Paul's voice I have no idea what he's talking about. Something about stimulating eggs and strong hormone injections. Jeremy is more skilled at retaining vast amounts of information, so hopefully he's absorbing all this and can relay the information to me at home. I now have the words 'strong hormone injection' reverberating in my mind. I hate hormones *and* injections, the combination sounds awful.

We're sent away with the first medication – injections, lovely – which will supress my menstrual cycle, which does actually sound lovely. I don't even try to administer the first injection myself – I can barely look at the needle – but Jeremy seems more than happy to do the honours and "stab me", his way of keeping this light and making me laugh. And despite the minor ordeal I'm feeling fantastic. This is it. It's happening.

We keep going with the injections every day for two weeks, following which my uterus is scanned and deemed 'fit for purpose'. We celebrate my functioning uterus with a trip to Golden Dragon for dinner before commencing on the next round of injections which will stimulate egg production.

With each daily injection I'm willing my body to produce follicles. Apparently it's follicles that I need – the little sacks that grow and release eggs – at least two or three of them, though ideally more. I'm feeling bloated and exhausted through the process and a bit emotionally on edge, but hope is so palpable I feel able to cope with anything. And I feel reassured by the fact that my body is reacting – it must be all those follicles I'm producing. It's a tiring business, follicle growing.

A scan after ten days shows I've produced seven follicles. I'm ecstatic. It's all going so well. I'm told to administer a 'trigger injection' in four days' time, thirty-six hours before egg retrieval, to help the eggs mature and then return to the clinic for egg harvesting. The big event.

We arrive at the clinic early and sit in silence watching the fish.

I'm nervous again. Worried about my eggs. Worried I might have wee-ed them out or something. Biologically impossible I know, but I'm still worried that something might have happened to those follicles and I'll be eggless and childless forever.

Jeremy has to go off somewhere to provide his sperm sample. I feel more nervous now I'm on my own. I notice one of the fish isn't moving and watch it intently for the next few minutes. It still hasn't moved. I'm now worried for the fish as well as my eggs and wonder whether I should mention something to the receptionist – about the fish, not my eggs – but I'm not sure whether she'd care (lots of people don't care about fish, I'm not even sure I do, so I don't know why I'm getting all stressed about this one). We're called in before I decide what to do about the fish and I promptly forget about it while I'm prepped for the procedure.

The anaesthetist is gentle. He moves and speaks slowly and I feel myself relaxing even before I'm sedated. Another injection. And then it begins to kick in; my body feels heavy, even my eyelids. I'm so relaxed I could sleep, but I will myself to stay alert. Everything is dimmed, blurred. Everything is on mute. I don't feel like I'm in my body.

CHAPTER 4 – Uncharted territory

Clare

I'm lying with my legs apart – as you would for a smear test – awaiting the momentous implantation. It's very undignified. I think I'd rather be sedated, as I was for the egg retrieval last week, despite the fact that I had felt unbearably sick and disoriented afterwards.

The process of collecting eggs took about half an hour, but it felt like seconds to me. My tummy ached when I came round; strange internal pains, which were momentarily disconcerting as I struggled to remember where I was or what was happening, as if I was emerging from a deep dream. But the discomfort didn't seem to matter so much when Jeremy told me they retrieved twenty-three eggs. Twenty-three! I kept forgetting this memorable piece of information as we drove home – dizzy from the motion and only half with-it – repeatedly asking Jeremy if they managed to get any eggs. He found my continual surprise and elation amusing and then a tad irritating, so wrote '23 eggs' on my hand when we got home.

The next day we had a call to say that from the eggs we left floating around in a petri-dish with Jeremy's sperm, seven were fertilised. Initially I wasn't sure what to think. Just seven? But Jeremy reminded me this is really good. Seven potential babies. The next few days were agony as we waited for the fertilised eggs to reach blastocyst –

early embryo form – hoping that they'd make it to day five and optimum maturity. I felt I'd left part of me, part of us, back at the clinic. All we could do was wait, hope, pray from a distance. None of it within our control.

But then, three days later, the news that only one made it. One. Twenty-three eggs. Seven fertilised. But only one embryo. I teetered on the edge for a moment, toying with slipping into panic or despair. But caught myself. *One* made it. That's all we need. Just one. And I couldn't help but feel that this must be *the one*. The embryo that will grow; the baby we'll know.

So now we're back at the clinic, with me in this undignified position, waiting to receive our future baby. We've been building up to this moment. We watch on a screen as the embryo goes in. There's silence for a moment as we wait. And then, voila. Done. It's weirdly anticlimactic. I make myself decent and we go home, feeling listless. What now?! I lie down as instructed and turn on the telly, flicking to Channel 4. Friends: 'The one where Chandler takes a bath'. Rachel is pregnant in this episode, she sneakily finds out the sex of the baby without telling Ross. I've always thought we'd keep the sex of our baby a surprise, but now I'm wondering if I'll be like Rachel, unable to resist finding out.

The next two weeks are excruciatingly long. I'm so tempted to take a pregnancy test, but have been instructed to wait for two weeks, so I do, battling to distract myself. Mabel the bike gets a break and I lie down as much as possible when I'm not at work. I've never felt so protective over my body. I'm tired and emotional, bawling my eyes out in the episode where Rachel has her baby. But I take this as a good sign. Pregnancy hormones. Must be.

I'm feeling confident when I eventually wee on the stick. In all the years of taking these tests I've never had a negative one. It's been a consistent rhythm of pregnancy for a few months, miscarriage, body recovering, a period or two and then pregnancy again. I put the stick to one side and try not to look at it. *Leave it for the full three minutes*, I tell myself, keeping busy by trimming my fingernails. But I do one nail, then look. The control line's there. I look away. Back to my nails. Another nail trimmed. I look again. Still just the control line. Where's the second line? It's not even faint. I'm starting to panic. Three minutes later and there is still just one line. Negative. *Negative?* I take another test, something must be wrong with this one. But this one is negative too. And the next. I'm crushed. 'Dreams do come true', I've been told. 'This is the year', I've been told. 'Pray in faith and it will be given to you', I've been told. 'Miracles happen', I've been told.

But not for us, so it seems.

The daffodils are majestic. It's a shame they're in the middle of the roundabout, so we can't stop and appreciate them. Or sneakily pick a couple. We're off to church but I don't want to go. It's Mothering Sunday and I find it painful to think about Mum at the moment. She's been steadily deteriorating and they say there's nothing more they can do for her. So, of course, we pray for a miracle healing. But I'm not sure I can do it anymore. I can't bring myself to pray such a bold prayer and face it not happening; the magnitude of heartbreaking loss heaped with confusion, disillusionment and a breakdown in my worldview. I can't do it. My prayers are ambiguous. Wordless. More like incoherent feelings offered up than anything I can make sense of or utter aloud.

We're going to drive down and visit Mum after the service. Each time I see her something's changed. I worry what state I'll find her in next. She's very composed about it all, to us at least. I have to find out how she's really doing via Dad. I don't know why she still protects us – habit I guess. I wonder what it feels like – that innate, uncontrollable, animalistic drive to protect your children. I wouldn't know.

In contrast to my mood, church is extra jubilant today. We meet in a massive warehouse, decked out with lights and a stage. It's flashy and professional, but also honest and heartfelt. I feel deep fondness for the place and the people who gather here, but I'm not sure where I fit anymore – too old to be a 'young adult', too childless to be included with the families. Floating somewhere in between. A bit of an outsider.

I struggle to connect with the hand raising and flag waving. A lump forms in my throat at the declarations of God's victory in our lives. But the topic of Mother's Day is approached with sensitivity; the motherless and childless are all considered with love and concern, which I'm grateful for. At one point in the service the children come round with a flower for all the women – again, sensitive – I accept my daffodil and hold it lightly. My mind wanders during the sermon. I'm here, but not.

There's a tap on my shoulder at the end, when everyone's milling around. "Clare." It's the lovely Sheila – older, motherly, perceptive. "For you." She hands me a bunch of daffodils, a look of acute empathy on her face. She leans in, tenderly. It's a big bunch. I'm wondering what I've done to deserve these. Does she think my mum has died?

"Oh!" I manage, "Thank you, Sheila."

"One for every baby lost." She pauses. "You're also a mother, Clare."

Her tenderness catches me. Tugs. It's physically painful. I feel it in my throat, in my chest, in my temples. It's so intense I don't know how to respond. It's such a thoughtful gesture. I feel seen. But the kindness hurts. It's too much. I have nowhere for this to go. No space for these invasive feelings I'm desperate to hold at bay. I want to scream, but I smile. I want to drop the flowers, but I hold them. Swallow.

"Thank you." I manage. I need to leave. But she offers to pray. I sense this is coming – and I accept out of politeness. But I'm nervous – even more nervous of other people's prayers than my own. Nervous of what she might claim; what theology she might impose that would jar with my experience or evoke anger that I have no energy to feel. But her prayer is child-like. Her words are few. She acknowledges my feeling of abandonment; she doesn't attempt to give uninvited shape or meaning to my experience. She simply asks, *"Lord God, draw near."*

Six months pass, during which we pick ourselves up and prepare mentally and emotionally for round two of IVF. Or attempt to. In reality the 'preparation' looks like me wanting to prepare but having no idea how. I can't forget my lived experience, conjure courage or dissipate anxiety. So I get back on Mabel the bike, re-commit to my liquid diet, and take on extra projects at work to keep myself distracted. Rebecca – one of my support group friends – had a successful first round and is not far off her due date. Confirmation that this can work. Another timely dose of hope.

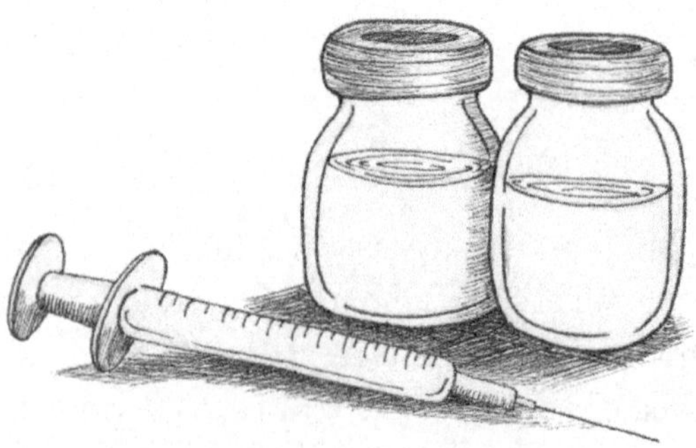

We begin our frequent trips to the clinic and daily injections. I find this round more gruelling. I have hope, but it's a little thinner on the ground, which makes being stabbed every day with a needle and the associated hormones harder to deal with. I convince myself I'm doing ok, but in reality I'm an emotional mess. Jeremy made some comment about stepping on eggshells around me. It was one of those jokes that is meant to convey a serious message. I didn't find it very funny – despite it being a fair comment.

I could say the same thing about him though; Jeremy's also on edge at the moment, still processing the disappointment of round one, and finding it harder to emotionally invest in this one. I think he's guarding himself a bit; monitoring his expectations, holding himself at bay. He's also pretty busy at work, now full-time with the charity linked to our church, attempting to bring some business strategy from all his years in the corporate sector to their information systems. It can be hard for him to get away for all the appointments.

They get eighteen eggs from me this time. I allow myself to feel pleased, but I'm careful with my emotions. There's less euphoria. Then nine fertilise. I allow myself to feel a little bit more. More embryos than last time. This is good. Then two make it to blastocyst. *Two*. Two potential babies. And they both make it to day five – an encouraging level of maturity. Hope rises. It's an addiction. I can't help it. They're both placed inside me, and two weeks later I get a positive test. Three positive tests, just to be sure. It's happening.

The next few weeks are excruciatingly slow. I keep making silly mistakes at work – my head's not in the game. And I attempt to strike a balance between rest and distraction, constantly worrying that I'm not resting enough, but then feel restless as soon as I stop. I keep thinking of a story I read on one fertility clinic's website; it was about a failed round of IVF being attributed to too much stress in the patient's life. My life needs to be stress-free. But I can't control anxiety. It creeps in. An uninvited foe. My constant companion.

Somehow we muddle through to seven weeks, distracting ourselves with celebrating my birthday – as is now traditional, I ask Jeremy for a baby, but he buys me a two-foot tall stone statue of a nude man for the garden instead, which would seem a bit of a wild, outlandish present to most, but I love it. I'm still getting a positive pregnancy test and we have our seven week scan today. My first scan.

I'm lying on the bed, jumper up, jeans pushed low on my hips. The sonographer puts gel on my tummy. It's cold. I'm drumming my fingers restlessly on the side of the bed. My heart beating fast. The probe is on my tummy now and there is an indistinct image on the screen. The sonographer is looking intently, jamming the probe hard into my stomach, moving it around. I'm looking at the screen. Squinting. Trying hard to find a baby in the fog of black and white lines, like looking for a shape in the clouds that is there one minute and gone the next. Why does nothing look like a baby? Why isn't she saying anything?

"Ok. Let me have a look down here," she moves the probe lower. "Maybe? Somewhere here... ah!" She looks visibly relieved. I exhale loudly. Thank God.

"Where?" I say, eagerly. Anxiously. I still can't make anything out. Though maybe that large blob could be a head?

"Here," she points at the screen. "You can see their body... here. And a head..."

"So glad it's got a head," Jeremy interjects. I laugh, making the image on the screen jiggle.

"Oh, try and stay still," she pleads, not laughing. "And you can just make out a tiny leg here. And an arm... here. And..." She pauses for a while. Frowning.

"Everything ok?" Jeremy asks after a minute.

"Well, yes! There's another one," she smiles, moving the probe slightly. "They're tucked behind this one, so they're quite hard to make out. But there are definitely two babies."

Two babies.

We leave the clinic, shocked but euphoric. I'm flooded by an old, familiar feeling – an absent friend, gone for too long – hope. It's so strong I can physically feel it in my body. Its energy. I tingle. This hope is so strong, confident, invasive, that I can't help but lean into it, embrace it. I want to monitor it. Temper it. Be realistic and measured. But it's too late. By the end of the drive home I'm all in. *This is it.*

I keep thinking back to a conversation I had with Mum last Sunday, sat by her bedside. "When I see God face to face, hopefully soon," she'd said, and I'd swallowed hard, not ready to face the reality of her not being here. "I'm going to ask him to give you a baby," she'd added, taking my hand and searching for my eye contact. She was so earnest. She believes wholeheartedly that she will meet her creator; that she will be more than spirit, able to speak; that God will care about what concerns her and be able and willing to respond. I cried in the moment, more at the thought of Mum being elsewhere than the prospect of her impending conversation with the divine. I was dubious about the latter. But I'm thinking about it again and it's feeding my hope.

As the weeks go by, hope is morphing into excitement. Anticipation. It's frighteningly uncontrollable. I'm starting to readdress the tentative plans I made six years ago during the early weeks of my first pregnancy; allowing myself a sneaky peak in Mothercare, window-shopping the prams, rubbing the soft fabric of a Babygro between my thumb and forefinger. I'm thinking about baby names. I love flower names – Daisy, Poppy. And Christabella, or Bella, after Mum. Or for a boy, William, after Jeremy's father and grandfather.

Jeremy is cautioning me, but I can tell he's also sliding. The temptation to indulge in this tantalising hope is too much. I can't resist. My soul, my body, need this.

I calculate a possible due date and put a small dot in the calendar. I'm clearly not confident enough to circle the date. However far gone I am in believing that this is happening, I'm still impatient to get to twelve weeks. Impatient to get to get past the first trimester. Impatient to get to my next scan and see them again. Impatient to get into new, unchartered territory. Everyone we know is praying for us. Hoping with us.

At the back of my mind I keep thinking about my twin who was stillborn. I keep thinking of us – me and my sister – early embryos in mum's womb, like the two inside me now. I'm willing them to live. History can't repeat itself.

I'm curled up on the couch with Borric, enjoying a moment of nothingness after having driven down to Petersfield to see Mum for the day, popping over to Alton to see Carol and the kids too. I want to be around Carol a lot at the moment. The dread of Mum's deterioration is hard to bear alone. We don't talk about it when we're together, me and Carol, but it simply feels good to be with her, knowing we feel the same – or similar.

Jeremy and I have been talking about moving in with Mum and Dad for a bit, to support Dad and be with Mum through this next season. I have no idea what to expect, what to hope for, what to believe. I am terrified of how I might feel. Right now I'm feeding off the adrenaline of driving back and forth to see her; keeping family updated and finding random ways to support. Busyness and distraction are essential – I need them in order to function at the moment. But I also need to rest right now. I need to be slow enough to listen to my body; to know what I need. To be intuitive towards these tiny lives inside me.

They're ten weeks now.

I peel myself off the couch and head for the fridge. "I need a little *something...*" I say to Jeremy, who's at the sink doing the washing up.

"My sumptuous dinner not enough for you?!" he replies, teasingly.

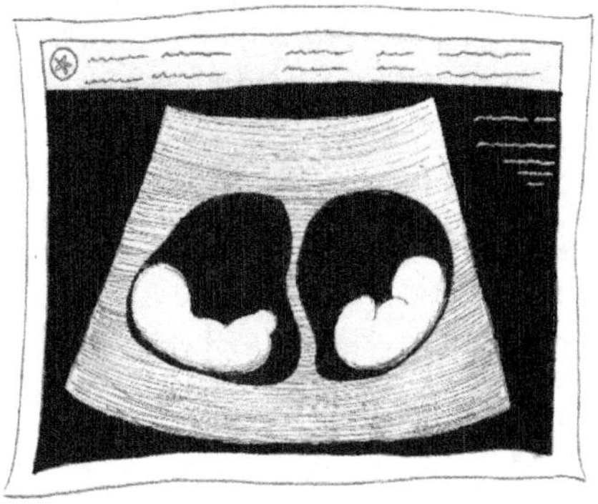

We've pinned the scan pictures on the door of the fridge and I pause and look at them before opening it – taking in their tiny figures, imagining how they've changed. I wonder what they look like now?

"They're the size of apricots," I say aloud.

"Huh?" Jeremy looks over his shoulder and catches me looking at the scan pictures. "Oh! The babies." He dries his hands on his trousers as he walks over to me, slipping him arms around my waist and kissing my cheek. We stay there for a moment, looking at the scan pictures in silence. Soaking in our reality.

"What do you fancy then?" He says eventually, giving me another kiss and heading back to the sink. "Some after dinner cheese and biscuits?"

I don't reply, opening the fridge and staring absent-mindedly at its contents. I don't know how long I stand there, lingering in the glow of the cold fridge light. My body feels odd. There is something perturbingly familiar about the sensation. This morning there was a small amount of browny-red substance on the tissue when I wiped after going for a wee. But it was brown, not bright red. And a small amount of discharge early in pregnancy is normal.

"You're letting all the cold air out!" Jeremy calls.

I shut the fridge, open the freezer, and grab the ice cream tub, deciding to ignore the unsettling feeling. "Ice cream!" I declare. "I fancy mint choc chip ice cream."

"No surprise there then!" he laughs.

I don't sleep well that night. Too much ice cream? Too much on my mind? In the past I would have flicked the light on, grabbed some paper and made a list of the things plaguing me. Getting them off my mind and on to paper. But they used to be things I could list – work tasks I'd forgotten about, someone's birthday I needed to remember. These days the things on my mind can't be listed. They're incoherent, lacking form; fragmented thoughts and feelings that move through my mind at such speed I can't catch them. There are no words for them.

It's so still and silent – other than Jeremy's deep breathing – but I'm restless. Toss. Turn. On the edge of sleep. My dreams are senseless and disconcerting – a reflection of my mind. Perhaps my body knows what's coming.

At two in the morning, it starts. A flood of warm blood. I lie still for a moment. *God, no.* I cannot be in this moment. But I am. I slide out of bed to the bathroom, leaving the light off. The darkness is a refuge. I don't want to see.

I bite into my hand as the cramps come. Although they're not like cramps, they feel more like what I've imagined contractions to be. "Jeremy!" I call out. *"Jeremy!"* He's there by my second cry. Appearing in the doorway and rushing to my side. Crouching beside me. Telling me it's ok.

Each time my uterus contracts, blood gushes. I sob. Undignified. Unreserved. Snot and tears mingle. And at one point I feel it; the moment one of our babies leaves my body. I know it's happened. I wonder whether to look, but I don't. I'm paralysed. I can't move.

I don't know how long we stay here. It feels like hours. We sit in silence, Jeremy's arms around me, listening to the sound of the boiler. It's still dark, just the light from the landing leaking round the cracks in the door. I often leave the landing light on – a comfort thing. But right now the darkness is more comforting than the light. I don't want to step into it, the light. I want to stay in my hidden place, away from reality.

Another wave hits me. It's not cramps this time, but I wonder whether the physical pain is comparable. It's hard to identify where the pain is coming from: my head, my temples, my throat, my chest. I cry silently, then loudly. Heaving. Giving into it. My cries mingle with Jeremy's. Surrendering to the pain.

We both take the next day off work. The bleeding continues and I try and get some sleep; moving between the toilet and my bed. Jeremy sits with me and brings me ice cream and other treats. We don't talk much.

I ring the IVF clinic and speak to a nurse, explaining that I'm miscarrying. She's sympathetic, but tells me to wait a couple of days and then take a pregnancy test. She also advises I see my GP and get my bloods done, I assume to confirm I'm miscarrying. The conversation is short, she must get this a lot.

When I take the test I can't look at it, giving it to Jeremy to confirm that it's negative. I see the GP a couple of times, who explains that the hormone levels in my blood tests are dropping, another indicator that I'm no longer pregnant. We make the necessary calls – Mum, Carol, Pat, Rachel. And message umpteen friends from church who have been praying and saying they have a 'good feeling' about this one, to tell them – in not so many words – that their 'good feelings' were unsubstantiated.

Jeremy goes back to work. I'm tempted to take more time off – people keep telling me that I should – but I don't know what to do with myself at home so I rock up at the office. I'm there, but I feel absent. My colleagues ask how things are going – they know I'm having IVF – so I tell them and they say, "oh... I'm so sorry. Is there's anything I can do..." and I say, "Thank you. We'll be ok," and smile and then sit down at my desk and stare at my screen. And then go home and try to have a nice time hanging out with Jeremy, but we're both annoyed at small things, like we don't know what the other needs. I'm annoyed that he can't intuitively know what I need, but then again I don't know what I need myself, so how on earth should *he* know? And nothing is right at the moment. No action, or gesture. It's too much or too little. I'm impossible.

So I go to bed, annoyed with myself, and toss and turn and get up early. I go down to the canal when no one is around and scream out loud, startling the birds; imposing my turmoil on the tranquillity. Upsetting the status of things.

At the weekend we go to the garden centre and buy two plants – bright red Cornus. One for each baby. We plant them in the garden. The ritual is helpful. The digging. The planting. And we stand there, spades in hand, and look at these plants, the tentative February sun gentle on our backs.

The following week at the IVF clinic they scan me, "just to check..." I find it excruciating. Of course, there are no babies, but the sonographer seems to feel the need to confirm this. Everyone is very nice about it, but I feel stifled and short of breath. I hate it.

We're advised to go back at the fertility clinic and check in with the consultant before pressing on with round three of IVF – the thought of which is almost unbearable at the moment. I have nothing left. How can we possibly go through it all again? But we dig deep and head to the consultant's clinic determined – determined to be heard. Determined to get some answers.

As expected, we don't see the consultant himself. I'm beginning to wonder if he actually exists. But the junior doctor we see is warm and attentive, listening intently as we explain about the second round of IVF and the fact that I lost the foetuses at ten weeks. Again, ten weeks. The same story.

"Something is wrong with me," I say with urgency. I need to be heard. "I don't think it's a fertility thing, we *can* get pregnant. My body just can't keep hold of the babies." I've lost count of the number of times I've said this. I almost feel like shouting it. Somebody hear me!

He's nodding. "I think we need to do some further tests, don't we?" he says.

His words are like honey.

"*Yes*," Jeremy says firmly. "We need to understand what's happening and what we can do next," He's leaning forward. His hand in mine. I'm swelling with hope. My heart like a hummingbird.

"The next step would be to send you for genetic tests. We're going to find out what's wrong before you embark on the next round of IVF." He makes a note of something on his PC before pushing his chair back from the desk. "I'll be back in a moment," he adds, no doubt off to get approval from the powers that be.

He's dangled something beautiful in front of us. The prospect of answers; the prospect of tailored medical help. This could be what we need. We wait in silence. Suspended.

CHAPTER 5 – It's just us

Jeremy

A wasp is buzzing in the corner of the windowpane, trying to escape. I'm wondering whether to use a magazine to help guide it out of the gap where the window is ajar, or just squish it. The buzzing is mildly irritating. As is Clare's foot-tapping and random chatter – she keeps repeating herself, going over what the doctor just said as if I wasn't in the room with her and hypothesising about what this might mean.

The atmosphere around us and between us is odd; relief and optimism mixed with ambiguity and anticipation. It's palpable. We've just been told we can have more tests done. Finally, a chance to find out what's going on; why the repeated miscarriages, why the apparent inability to carry a baby to term. But the doctor left the room before elaborating. So I'm sitting here with my questions, restless to know more. What would these genetic tests involve? When can they start? What is the wait time on the NHS? What are they looking for?

Clare has fewer questions, if any. She's succumbed to hope despite the risks and keeps saying how amazing this is. *Someone has understood*, I agree and I'm so relieved. But I need to find out more and I'm impatient to lock in this offer of more tests.

The door opens and a man strolls in. It must be *him* – the elusive consultant. I sit up, as I would have done when the headmaster entered a room when I was in prep school. He's smaller than I imagined; a bald head, beard and monobrow. He perches on the edge of the desk. He clearly doesn't intend to stay long, but I'm encouraged – the big dog's here. This has got to be good. We finally get to discuss our issues with the decision maker.

"I gather you've had two failed rounds of IVF and are wanting further tests done to find out why?" He launches straight in. No introductions. I notice the junior doctor has just slipped in behind him and is standing awkwardly to the side. He'd seemed so self-assured moments ago; but he's small and uncertain now his authority is being usurped.

"Yes, that's right," I shift in my chair. His commanding presence is making me feel uncomfortable, possibly inferior. It's a relatively foreign feeling; one I intentionally parked in my twenties. Another twenty years on and I'm not used to my confidence being this easily derailed. I almost add 'Sir', but refrain.

"Doctor...er." I look over at the junior doctor, his name evading me.

"Martin." He fills in. He doesn't look thrilled at being drawn into the conversation.

"Yes, sorry. Doctor Martin just suggested that we should have some tests done as we're having problems with recurrent miscarriage. We want to see if we can find out what's going on before we start on the third round of... "

"There won't be a third round." The consultant interjects.

"Sorry, er..." I'm not following.

"We'll be cancelling the final round of IVF." There's a pause. The wasp is buzzing frantically. "And we won't be doing any further tests." He adds.

"Sorry," I say again. I don't know why I'm apologising or what I'm apologising for. "I'm confused. We're um..." I've never felt so ineloquent, but words are evading me.

"The problem is that she's overweight." He says bluntly, nodding in Clare's direction.

"*Clare*," I add firmly. I'm hot with alarm. He needs to use her name.

But he doesn't pick up on this. He presses on, insensitivity swelling. "That's clearly the problem here. Her BMI is too high."

She's in the room, why is he talking about her as though she's not here? I'm appalled. How *dare* he pin all our heartache on Clare. He knows *nothing*. I'm bound by British politeness that keeps me in my chair, physically restraining me from getting up and shaking him. Clare hasn't made a sound.

"Clare's BMI has been within the requirements for each round," I'm louder now, and more assertive. But he doesn't hear.

"We'll be cancelling the third round," he's addressing Doctor Martin now. "And no need for the tests." He looks at his watch. "I have a meeting now."

As he leaves the room I wonder if he has any idea of the destruction he's leaving in his wake.

We rush to book in for our final round of IVF, aware that the archaic cogs of the NHS administrative system will work in our favour. By the time anything's been officially cancelled and logged in the system, we'll be well underway with the final round.

This decision required little to no discussion. We're in agreement that the consultant's assessment was ill-informed and unfounded, and despite our exhaustion and hesitancy, we know we need to try again. This last round of IVF feels like our last chance. But I never imagined we could leave the fertility clinic more discouraged than we were when we arrived. We were teetering on the edge of feeling demoralised when we walked through the doors; our emotions were toyed with and hopes raised, only to leave utterly crushed. We're compelled to keep going, but to do so while feeling misunderstood and unsupported by those who have power to make decisions about our future feels lonely and exhausting.

I'm hyper-aware of Clare; worried about how she's processing the consultant's accusation. It's essential that she doesn't shoulder this burden. None of this is her fault and I'm still reeling at the audacity of the consultant insinuating that it is. We need to box his comments and file them as inaccurate and unfortunate. But I feel a sense of panic at having been so controlled by someone else's uninformed assessment. The hope of finding out what is really going on has been snuffed out. I'm struggling to know how to keep the remaining embers burning; running out of fuel and devoid of hope-filled energy.

But a few months later we resume a sort of trance-like autopilot. Clare's back on Mabel the bike and a liquid diet, despite her BMI being within the requirements for IVF, and I'm back to injecting her with hormones every evening. I try to make light of it, but nothing about this situation is remotely amusing. I think back to the first round, recalling the excitement and anticipation – how every injection, every appointment was heaped with progress and optimistic expectation. This time we're crawling through, disillusioned and bone-deep tired with it all.

Meanwhile Chris is rapidly deteriorating, and we decide to decamp down to Petersfield to support Mike as he cares for her. So the stress of IVF is compounded by living with my in-laws, surrounded by nicknacks and a wife and father-in-law who are running on adrenaline to hold grief at bay. I'm a tad nervous around Clare. She seems to be doing ok; showing signs of rationality, humour and positivity. But then she melts, or snaps, unexpectedly. She's unpredictable; an emotional loose cannon. Everything in her life is out of control. I'm trying to contain it and hold it for her. But I'm at a loss. I resort to practicalities – keeping Mabel well oiled, driving Clare to the clinic when she's tired, cooking dinner. These things are as much to keep me going as to keep her supported. I must not crumble.

They retrieve nine eggs this time. Clare is even more disoriented than previous occasions when she comes round from the procedure; perhaps she gave into the sedation as welcome relief from reality. I have to provide a sperm sample again – my only part in the process. I find it awkward and humiliating, sitting in a small cubicle with a pot and magazines to "assist". It's a small ask – enduring a dose of awkwardness as opposed to weeks of injections, hormonal changes, fluctuating moods, and medical procedures. But I hate it nonetheless and feel relieved that this is the last time I have to do it.

We leave a bit of ourselves behind again and then distract ourselves with work, Chris' needs or the latest season of Homeland. Generally, we're leaving the hoping and praying to other people; it feels like an impossible emotional investment for us right now.

Clare's a sharer – usually wearing her heart on her sleeve – so everyone knows this is the last round. If it had been left to me I wouldn't have told anyone about our IVF journey; I'd have gone through the entire thing just us. It's intensely painful and private. I want to draw a circle around it, carefully monitoring who, if anyone, can enter or even sit at the circumference. This is not for others to see, or comment on, or emotionally participate in. Anyone else in this space seems to add to the level of risk. But I appreciate that for Clare, it helps to share the pain. Inviting others to walk the road with her lifts the load. So I let her do the sharing and updating, and if I'm asked I say the basics; that we're on the last round of IVF and that we're doing ok. One is fact, the other denial.

"This better work," Clare says a few weeks later when the one embryo that made it to blastocyst is implanted. Hope has morphed into something that resembles bitter resolve and determination. We're weathered; fighting not to give in to cynicism.

We visit my family down in Somerset for the weekend. My parents moved to be closer to my sister, Rachel and her husband David. They have four kids now; Sam is eleven, Martha seven, Isaac three and Nancy's just turned one. It's chaos, but a welcome and much-needed distraction. My family seem to instinctively know how to rally around us; gently addressing our pain without stifling us with too many questions. We relax into their company and feel refreshed by the spring air, sea breeze and the beautiful garden my parents are busy transforming. The change of scene enables us to temporarily forget. Maybe we should move here? Embrace this feeling of newness?

Somehow the company of our nieces and nephews feels like pure gain rather than a reminder of what we're missing. But down on the beach, every small child frolicking in the sand reflects the cavernous hole in our reality. I cannot find a way of reimagining our future without children. "You'll be next," people say. But we're not. It's been ten years. And I have no idea how you go about letting go of a dream you never asked for. This desire for a family wasn't something we conjured, but something that laid hold of us and now won't let go. We welcomed it initially, its grip was gentle and exciting. But now we're trapped, held firm by a desire we can't fulfil.

We don't linger in Somerset, despite wanting to. Clare can't bear being away from her mum for too long, just in case. But Chris seems to be doing ok, even making it to Clare's cousin's wedding – tired and wheelchair bound, but present – and everyone says how well she's looking and how glad they are that she's improving.

Optimism swells with spring growth; Clare takes a pregnancy test and it's positive. We linger in the moment. Two lines on the wee stick; buds on the trees; Chris smiling, chatting and embracing life with the little energy she has left.

But the tentative hope evaporates. Three weeks later Chris dies. And two weeks after that Clare miscarries. Loss heaped on loss.

We're tender at the funeral. Our wounds open; yet to be dressed, unable to heal. I'm hoping no one in this sea of loving, well-meaning family and friends asks about how IVF is going. I would wince, or lie.

After the service is over we spill out of the church on to the steps outside, sipping coffee with the April sun on our faces, Chris lying in the hearse a few metres away. I stick close to Clare, observing her and trying to anticipate her needs. Although if I'm honest I'm at a loss. I have no idea what she needs or might need. This wilderness of grief is an unknown landscape.

But surprisingly, the atmosphere feels light right now, with everyone milling around, greeting one another, hugging and exchanging pleasantries. It's preferable to the heavy silence before the service; everyone filing in quietly, nodding at one another and then avoiding eye contact, absorbing themselves with their service sheets.

No one interacts with us for more than a minute or two; brief, pained comments, "I'm so sorry for your loss," or, "how lovely that the sun is out," and then they move on. One well-meaning cousin asks Clare how she's doing. An impossible question. Clare says she's doing "ok" – she's well versed in this answer. Aren't we all? In reality she's a million miles from ok, but how do you even begin to answer that vast question? And does anyone actually want an honest response?

Mike comes over and says it's time to follow the hearse to the crematorium. Clare goes into overdrive in the car, talking constantly, and making a terrible joke when we accidently hit a pigeon, laughing about how ironic it is that we've killed something at a funeral. I'm relieved it's only a five-minute drive, until I realise that the hearse is taking an unexpected detour. They seem to be doing a drive past Mike and Chris' house. I wonder if Mike requested this – it seems like an unnecessary emotional trigger. It's certainly a bit much for Clare, who falls silent for a moment, glancing at the house which is alive with memories of her mum (some just weeks ago). She shifts uncomfortably before turning the conversation to Auntie Margaret's blue hair.

The crematorium is an unfortunate building; dark and foreboding. Clare falls silent again on arrival. We sit at the front, eyes on the wicker coffin, centre stage. Clare put the scan pictures of the twins in the coffin with Chris. It was my suggestion. We needed them to go. To lay them down, give them up, rather than tuck them away to encounter again or suffer the daily reminder of their loss pinned on our fridge. I'd cried when we lost them. I was caught off guard by the physical pain – my tight, heaving chest, constricting throat, aching head. I was fighting against my body; my will to control myself overpowered by a greater, physical force. Looking at the coffin now – thinking of the barely formed babies we'd loved so intensely and Chris, whose quirky presence and loving kindness has been such a fundamental part of my life these past seven years – the same sensation encroaches on my body. The vicar is committing Chris' body, "Ashes to ashes, dust to dust." I swallow hard, releasing a long, slow exhale, looking at my shoes and regaining control and composure.

The red curtain parts to make way. And then she's gone.

Back outside, I slip my arm around Clare's waist and find myself instinctively asking the loaded question. "Ok?" I whisper. I don't know why I ask this. I know she's not ok, but she looks at me and manages a smile. And something about standing here together, in the sun, amidst the grief and loss, and Clare's weak smile, is a sense that we will be – to some extent – ok. And that one day we'll be able to answer that simple, loaded question with 'yes', and mean it.

We've stopped Googling about IVF and started trawling Rightmove instead. It's proving a helpful antidote to grief. Clare goes straight for the pictures and I scroll down to the details, looking at the structure, history and how long it's been on the market. We're searching within a thirty-mile radius of my parents' house in Somerset.

At one point the thought of leaving London, or the surrounding counties, would have been too much of an upheaval, but now a move feels bright and enticing. There is nothing tying us here anymore, especially now Chris has died. Clare had wondered about staying near her dad, for emotional support in the weeks and months following the funeral. But he became quickly preoccupied, spending lots of time with an old friend, Shirely, who he marries six months later, much to everyone's surprise, changing the nature of family dynamics on Clare's side. It's a lot for Clare and Carol to process, but ultimately everyone's pleased Mike has someone to do life with.

Neither Clare nor I are tied to an office anymore. In January I left the charity I was working for, setting up my own business offering an information management system for not-for-profit organisations. I need to be in London from time to time, but increasingly less. So, I keep finding myself wondering why we're still here; what is tying us to this physical place? A place heavy and evocative, indiscriminately triggering memories we're ready to leave behind.

We've been down to Somerset to view a few properties. There was one in particular that caught my attention. It had character; exposed beams, uneven floors, and two acres of land, with old barns that could house my vintage buses, currently residing in a barn in Hampshire I'm co-renting with my best friend, Bob. I had to persuade Clare to go and see it – perhaps it was the hideous internal décor that put her off. But once we were there in person – seeing past the lime green walls, heavily patterned carpet and mahogany furniture – she caught my vision for the place.

We put in an offer and get it for a steal, cracking open some red wine – even Clare has some – delighted to have something to celebrate. We are elated, yet grounded; finally asserting a level of control over our lives again.

I don't feel sentimental leaving our home in Berkhamsted. Neither does Clare, which surprises me – the emotional being that she is. This house has been the setting for such a significant part of our life; symbolic of our early years together and a refuge through so much trauma; the most recent being losing our beloved Borric – he was old in cat years, but we could have done without another loss. We absorb ourselves with the practicalities of packing, only slowing down and inadvertently taking a moment to reflect when digging up the flame-red Cornus we planted in memory of the twins.

I suggest to Clare that this could be an opportunity to slim things down and purge her bag collection, but not unexpectedly, she disagrees and packs every bag she's ever owned. She echoes this minimalist sentiment back to me when I'm sorting out the shed. I remind her that each tool serves an entirely different function. She says the same is true for her bags.

We're physically tired from the move, but emotionally energised. Everything's still in boxes, an overwhelming task, but it's absorbing, and the whole process is breathing life back into us. Clare's just eased open a can of white paint – she agonised over colours for weeks and then chose white – managing to flick it all over her face. She laughs and it strikes me that the sound is unusual. I feel like I'm getting her back. She tips the paint into a tray and begins rolling. A bit here and a bit there. There is nothing systematic about her painting style. I'm tempted to say something but resist, opting rather for grabbing my own roller and filling in her gaps.

Clare's put on Kylie Minogue, which I can just about tolerate. She's singing along to 'Chocolate', flicking more paint absent-mindedly as she busts out a few dance moves. Coben, one of two new feline friends, comes in mewing loudly, eyeing up the paint, followed closely by Deaver who makes a beeline for my roller. "Noooo!" Clare intercepts Deaver, scooping her up and staring out the window while I continue the hard labour.

"I don't feel so sad," she says, unexpectedly, following a few moments of silence.

"That's good." I don't know what else to say, but grab the remote and turn Kylie down a bit, indirectly inviting Clare to say more, should she want, which I suspect she might.

"It *is* good. But it also feels strange to not feel sad, if that makes sense." She pauses, still stroking Coben therapeutically. "I need to move forward, but I also don't want to. Like part of me wants to stay in my sadness. It's so familiar and seems to stand for everything I've lost. But it also feels like a relief to feel a bit of joy again."

She continues in the same vein and I try to piece together what she's saying. I want to rejoice in the retreating sadness, but appreciate that it's not that simple. Regardless, I share her tentative joy, and we continue to transform the walls from lime green to white.

A few months later we're starting to feel settled, despite still having so much to do. I'm in the outbuildings taking some measurements; stables which could be converted into offices and the large barns for my buses. I would need to rig up some enormous doors to the barns. I pull out a notepad, breathing on my fingers to get the blood flowing, and sketching down some ideas of how these could work. It's January now and bitterly cold.

I don't hear Clare come over. She makes me jump. She's been acting strangely today. Good strange, I think. Preoccupied, vacant and humming to herself. I ask her what she thinks of my idea for the barn doors. I'm mildly frustrated that she's not listening, but accept that ultimately she doesn't care about them and would agree with my idea, however outlandish.

"Something on your mind?" I probe. She shrugs mysteriously.

Despite better, more hopeful days, we're continually reminded that the journey of healing is complex; far from linear. The past few months have been up and down. I suspect these days will sit adjacent: the fresh, joy-filled days spent painting the house and exploring our new surroundings, alongside the disheartening uncovering of old emotions.

I frequently think about our encounter with the consultant in the fertility clinic. Unable to shake it, despite it being over a year ago now. I'm not usually one for dwelling on 'what ifs', but I can't help but wonder what might have happened, what we might have discovered, had he allowed us to go ahead with the genetic tests. What if they had found something? Could our story be different if we had just picked a different clinic and encountered a more understanding consultant? I circle through all these questions, like a necessary ritual, before landing back in our reality, accepting and embracing it as much as I can.

At least the lack of answers, the dead end to the question of why we don't seem able to have children, means that the problem remains *ours*. This is something we're in together. It's not because of something to do with Clare, or something to do with me, it's something we share; a joint problem, a mutual crisis. I know Clare has had moments of blaming herself – wondering if something is wrong with her, berating herself for her body's experience. But it's not her, it's us. It's *our* journey. This trauma could have pushed us apart, but it's doing the opposite.

The bigger challenge, so it seems, is readjusting our vision of the future. On three separate occasions this week we've been asked whether we have children – the downside of moving somewhere new. It's refreshing to feel anonymous, but hard when people are inquisitive and ask us questions we don't want to be asked. I guess it's an understandable question; we're of *that age* and seem to have moved to an area where there are a number of young families. I suppose we've also bought a family home, and it doesn't seem obvious to people that we bought it to give space for my buses and Clare's nude statue collection, rather than children. But however reasonable the question, we both find it painful and uncomfortable. A simple question knocking us sideways. I see Clare visibly slipping. Her expression changing, sometimes becoming even more animated to mask the welling up of distress underneath.

I wonder if we'll ever get to a point where we can say, "No, we don't have children", and feel happy with that statement. Or, "it's just us," and say it like it's something we've chosen rather than something that's happened to us. There are so many days when I'm overwhelmed with gratitude of how happy we can be, just us; grateful for how fun life is with Clare, for the adventures we've had together – Paris to Vancouver, Jamaica to Las Vegas – camping out under the stars, climbing mountains and exploring cities; content, encouraged and inspired in each other's company.

But I'm still baffled as to how we fully embed ourselves in the contentment we often feel when it's just us, and re-envisage the future without children. I'm not sure if it's possible. And it seems that somewhere, deep down in our subconscious, we still believe people when they say, "you'll be next." After all this time, how can we still harbour any hope of having a child? But we do.

Clare still hasn't given me any insight into her preoccupied mind. She's frowning at my very clear, to-scale drawings as if they're illegible.

"Clare?"

"Right, yes. My mind." She says, as if needing to clarify that she has one. "There is something on my mind." She's speaking slowly, suspiciously so. I'm starting to feel a little nervous. What's she hiding?

She puts the drawing down and looks at me. “There’s something I need to tell you.”

PART 2

2013–2019

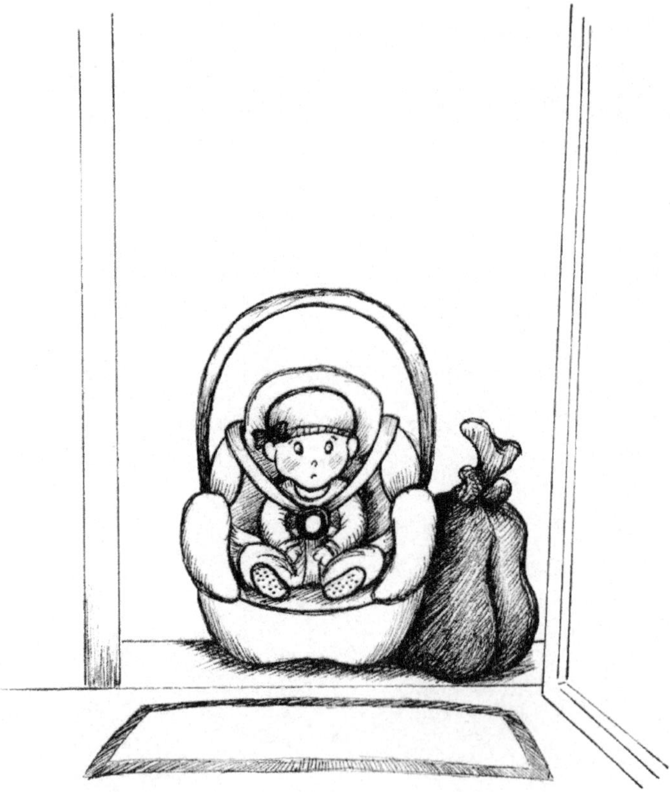

CHAPTER 6 – A precursor

Jeremy

"He still won't acknowledge me as his father."

The man standing at the front of the room says this in a calm, matter-of-fact way, as if it's the most ordinary thing to say about your son. A few people in the rows in front of us are shifting in their seats. It doesn't make for comfortable listening. Clare and I are sitting in the back row. There are perhaps forty-five people here – more than I expected – and we're about three-quarters of an hour into the evening, halfway through if they finish on time.

"It's been two years since he came into our lives," the man at the front continues. "Mostly we feel grateful that he's at least formed an attachment to one of us. And we were always aware that his history of abuse from his birth mother's partner might make it harder for him to trust men."

He pauses and takes a sip of water. I follow suit, taking a sip of coffee from the paper cup I'm holding. It's cold. I swallow it and place the cup under my chair, picking Clare's coat off the floor and draping it over the back of her chair.

"The aggressive behaviour has continued. It's usually directed towards me but we're witnessing some signs of self-harm too, which is really alarming and upsetting to see in a six-year-old."

Again, the matter-of-fact tone.

"Most of the time this involves scratching himself, digging his nails into his skin or biting himself. And a lot of screaming, often until he's hoarse. It's not uncommon for him to draw blood, especially if he's particularly upset about something. We're trying to identify his triggers and introduce calming activities before the moment gets out of control, but his emotional meltdowns can be pretty unpredictable. We know patience and consistency are key."

The man continues to talk about their 'gentle parenting style'; how traditional discipline and punishments tend to escalate the situation and how he and his wife always stop to think about the root cause of the emotional outburst or 'bad behaviour'. He makes quotation marks in the air with his fingers when he says 'bad behaviour' to make sure we know that this is not actually bad behaviour. It sounds pretty bad to me.

Just when I'm about to question the sincerity of this saint-like individual before me, who appears to deal with an exceptional amount of 'bad behaviour' with patience and good grace, he unexpectedly crumbles.

"It's been really tough," his voice is shaking. There's no more shifting in the rows ahead, everyone is still. I note how unusual it is to see a man show emotion in public.

"I was told to be honest with you, so... yeah," he takes a deep, slow breath and gathers himself. "It's been hard. We love him so much and we wouldn't go back. But we weren't prepared for the emotional weight and the strain it would put on our marriage."

He pauses, as if he might go on, but the woman who is compèring the evening comes up and thanks him, briefly placing a hand on his shoulder and giving him a reassuring smile. He thanks us for listening and takes his seat on the front row. There is a brief moment when we wonder if we should clap – I assume others are feeling the same as there is a solitary clap from somewhere in the room, followed by an awkward cough.

I glance at my watch. Another half an hour. It's been very enlightening, but significantly heavier than I was anticipating. This is the 'something' Clare had sheepishly told me about the other week; that she'd signed us up for an adoption information evening, hopping on the bandwagon of another agonisingly wild adventure before we've had time to recover from the last. She has a tendency to run with an idea once it starts forming in her head, however embryonic and unthought-through.

I probably would have let the idea sit for a bit longer before signing us up for something – read some books on adoption, subscribed to an adoption magazine, that sort of thing. I also would have allowed us more time to heal before embarking on something so monumentally huge. But, nevertheless, here we are at an adoption information evening run by the local council, sitting shoulder to shoulder with other prospective adoptive parents, and despite my reservations I'm rolling with it, aiming to stay open-minded.

A few other people share their experiences of adopting from the front – all men, which I find unexpected, especially having just emerged from the world of miscarriage and IVF, which was overwhelmingly female-centred – and the compère wraps up the evening, pointing us to forms on a table at the back of the room where we can register our interest to find out more. I already know that Clare will want to fill out a form.

She gathers her coat, scarf, hat, water bottle, keys, phone and whatever else she's stashed under her chair with unusual speed (I'm typically waiting five minutes for her to arrange herself) and says, "shall we...?" gesturing towards the table with her head and eyebrows in the absence of any available arms.

"Sure." We're not committing ourselves to anything, simply registering our interest. We're the first at the table and I fill out the form with some basic details.

Clare hands me her bundle of things as we leave the building, struggling with her coat and commenting on how cold it is. I light-heartedly remind her that it's January, and constantly cold, while inwardly marvelling at her continual surprise at the weather which seems to require regular comment. We get in the car and she blasts the heating.

"For an evening meant to *promote* something they were really trying hard to put us off!" Clare says, exhaling. I can tell she's exhausted by the experience. I listen as she goes back over the evening in great detail, as if I wasn't there. She goes round in circles, reminding me that there are loads of children currently in care and in need of 'forever homes' – over nine-thousand children to be exact, she's not a details person – and how it would be such a great thing to do, but could we manage it, it sounds so hard, but could also be so rewarding, and maybe we *should* as there is such high need, and did I see the man who nearly cried? – yes Clare, I *was* there.

"They kept saying how rare it is to be matched with a baby," she says, pausing from her monologue and turning the 'blasters', as she calls them, down while removing her coat – the car is now an oven and I'm sweating slightly. I've been waiting for her to mention this. We learnt this evening that even if a baby is taken into care, it can take years of court proceedings before it is deemed impossible for them to return to their birth parents, meaning that the youngest children up for adoption are usually toddlers. We've spent the last nine years of our life thinking about babies, getting our heads around not having one feels like a really big deal.

"Let's sleep on it," I say. "We're not in a rush."

"No," she agrees, "and they did say it could take a long time to go through the application process, so we might as well roll with it and then we've still got lots of time to reconsider and pull out."

It's not quite what I meant. I prefer to make firm, informed decisions before jumping in. We've expressed interest, not officially started the application process. But also I sense there's no slowing Clare down on this one.

"Let's talk about it again in the morning," I conclude. She's frustrated at me shutting down the conversation, but I know we're not going to get anywhere tonight. "We're unlikely to hear from social services for a few weeks. We've got plenty of time to talk."

Much to my surprise, and to social services' credit, they called the next week, and three days later they've dispatched a social worker to come and visit us.

We're standing in our dining room and the social worker – Stewart – is at the bottom of our staircase inspecting the banister.

"The gaps between the railings are a bit big," he says with concern.

"A bit big?" I repeat.

"Yes, a small child could fall between these." He's still looking at the banisters. Clare gives me a look of bewilderment which says, 'I tidy the house from top to bottom and he's looking at the banisters?!'

I'm even more caught off guard by this banister comment. I had expected this to be more of a formal conversation, an opportunity to ask some questions and find out more about adoption rather than a house inspection. I'd told Clare that her manic tidying and unpacking of the final boxes from our move had been over the top – we're just exploring things at the moment, not committing to anything. She's even thrown away the lingering dead flowers – her subtle hint to me to buy more – and washed the cats' food bowls (or bowels as she writes in her to-do list, the correct spelling always evading her).

There's a moment of silence. I hear the cat flap click. In comes Coben with a mouse hanging from his mouth. He's named after the author, Harlan Coben; famous for his callous murderers. It feels like an appropriate name right now. Clare looks horrified. I feel amused as he makes a beeline for Stewart and drops the mouse at his feet; cats have a way of finding the least cat-friendly person in the room.

It's just a gift, but Stewart doesn't appreciate it, gasping and retreating up the stairs as if the mouse is still alive. At the information evening they mentioned a number of times that it's not advisable to adopt if you have pets – something about jealousy and competing for attention. I hope this current situation doesn't stack against us in more ways than one. I grab some kitchen towel and pick up the mouse in one hand and Coben in the other, thanking him for bringing us a gift but explaining that mice need to stay *outside*.

"Jeremy likes to talk to the cats," Clare says to Stewart as I remove Coben, "he says it's the only intelligent conversation he gets round here! Rude!" She fake laughs. "*Anyway!* Would you like a tea or coffee, or something else to drink?"

By the time I've disposed of the dead mouse, adding it to the other twenty decomposing rodent bodies in the bin outside, and come back in, order is restored and Clare and Stewart are sitting in our living room chatting – this scene bears a closer resemblance to what I'd imagined.

He repeats a lot of what was shared at the information evening: that there are thousands of children in care needing 'forever homes'; that the process of adopting can be very drawn out, often taking years, and it can be very intrusive; that we wouldn't get placed with a baby and that the children needing to be adopted are often very damaged. In summary, his message was, 'we really need you to do this, but you really don't want to do this.' I suspect he's trying to figure out whether we're worth his time.

Everything feels fairly predictable until he asks to see upstairs. He's just told us the process is intrusive, so maybe this is a test?

"Of course," I say calmly, at the same time Clare says a loud, sharp, "why?" I know she didn't bother tidying upstairs.

"Oh, just to see if you have a big enough property. Enough bedrooms, that sort of thing."

We clearly have a big enough property, but I gingerly lead him upstairs, reminding him to be careful of the gappy banister on the way up. He takes a quick look around, and makes a note of something while I explain about the renovations we plan to do. He quizzes me in great detail about all the various DIY projects as we head back downstairs and I assure him they're all happening soon.

"There're lots of changes you would need to make to your garden as well," Stewart says as he leaves, taking the liberty of having a quick look up the drive and across to the barns where my buses are soon to be residing. "Like that fence," he gestures across the garden, "that's climbable, so you'd need to put chicken wire on the top. I'll need to get someone round to do a safety inspection on your property."

Chicken wire wasn't quite the aesthetic vision we had for our grounds, but then again Clare's nude statues are lowering the tone anyway.

He gets in his car and we stand at the door, smiling and waving.

"Sorry about the mouse!" Clare shouts as he backs out of the driveway.

Despite the fact that Clare has been a bit ahead of herself with all this, she says exactly what I'm thinking. "Wow. We've not even agreed to anything yet and they're already inspecting our house!"

She's right, the visit felt surprisingly specific and extreme; perhaps it's a precursor for what's to come.

CHAPTER 7 – Guinea pigs

Jeremy

It's been two months since we attended the information evening and things are moving quicker than anticipated. We keep reminding ourselves that we can back out at any point. Despite not being fond of putting off big decisions, this is a comforting thought. We're taking tentative steps forward while sitting on the fence. It's exactly what they don't want us to do; is this what being rebellious looks like in your forties?

We now have an assigned social worker, Jo. She's been coming round every week for the last five weeks. She sits on the brown sofa, always in the same spot, sometimes with a cat on her lap, and asks us probing questions about our relationship, our income, our sex life, our childhoods. We divulge all this information. Jo makes notes, asks more probing questions and then, after about an hour and a half, leaves. We're aware that ultimately she is the one who will fight our corner – advocate for us as prospective adoptive parents – and despite not knowing how committed we are to this venture, we're eager to come across well.

Jo's collating all the information she needs for a PAR – Prospective Adopters Report – which will be submitted to the adoption panel to support our application to become adoptive parents. We will then sit in front of this panel – made up of social workers, a medical advisor, and a number of independent members who bring unique skills and experiences to the panel (including an adoptive parent and someone who has been adopted) – and they will ask us questions about our PAR and ultimately deem whether we're suitable parent material or not.

"It's sort of like therapy but not," Clare says one evening, sprawled on the sofa after a Jo-visit, eating mint choc chip ice cream out of the tub and half-watching Friends. I think about her comment without answering. It doesn't feel very therapeutic; it's repetitive and rigorous, often leaving us feeling emotionally spent. But then again, we're being asked to open up in the way you would to a therapist, laying bare intimate details about our lives, reflecting on our least favourite memories of childhood. And Jo, although formal and focused, has therapist-like tendencies. She's approachable, genuinely interested in us and clearly very good at what she does, gently and seamlessly guiding us through a myriad of questions and tasks.

"Except I'm guessing a therapist would listen and not judge," I say eventually, "but we're being judged on everything we say..." My sentence trails off and we sit in silence for a moment, turning our attention back to Friends and thinking about how absurd the adoption process feels at times.

There is a sense in which we're being coached, like witnesses rehearsing a testimony before they stand up in court. If we say something Jo isn't sure about, she'll continue questioning us until our answer conforms. Clare recalls being smacked from time to time as a child; she hesitated when Jo asked her if she would ever smack a child, I guess she'd never thought about it before. Jo went to great lengths to ensure Clare arrived at the right answer for her paperwork: that of course she would never smack a child, neatly correlating with the local council's stance on smacking. Despite both of us being happy with this 'final answer' and ultimately feeling aligned with everything Jo is writing down, it sometimes feels like being expertly coerced into making decisions we've not had the chance to think about independently. Clare's taken to responding with what she considers to be humorous answers when the atmosphere gets a bit intense.

"The 'I'd lock the children in the cupboard if they got too much' comment was an unfortunate one, Clare," I say, amused at the recollection of Clare's blunder and Jo's horrified look. "You were certainly judged on your bad joke!"

"Oi, *Wilson.* I was *being funny*!" Clare throws a cushion at me. "Trying to lighten the mood a bit, you know. Does it all need to be quite so intense?"

We're quiet for a moment, turning our attention back to Friends in time to hear Chandler addressing a door, "I'm funny, right...? What would you know? You're a door. You only like knock knock jokes..." Clare laughs, despite having watched this episode countless times.

I'm thinking about her question, which I know she doesn't need or want me to answer. Does it need to be so intense? It's partly Jo's style, she's very professional – which I like, it's reassuring – but it's also the topics we're discussing. They are by nature intense. Today we had to complete a tick-box exercise, indicating which children we are willing to adopt. It felt brutal. *Would you adopt a child who was the product of rape? A child who was blind? A sibling group?* Clare and I would look at each other, trying to come to a telepathic agreement. We had no warning about this exercise, no time to discuss in advance.

So far, most of the Jo-visits have been focused on us; our background, our support network, our health. It was an unexpected gear change when Jo whipped out this questionnaire. She seemed particularly interested in the instances when we disagreed; Clare leaning more frequently towards 'yes, we'd take any child' and me asking a lot of questions. When we got to, *Would you adopt a child with additional needs*, I'd asked Jo to elaborate. Were we talking about a child with dyslexia or a child with more complex needs, requiring constant assistance and support? We probably couldn't manage the latter, we reflected out loud, but decided to say 'yes' anyway as the question felt too vague to give a categorical 'no'.

Whenever we arrived at a 'no' – as with, *a child in a wheelchair* – we felt compelled to give a reason. In this instance we agreed our house couldn't be adapted for a wheelchair – too many different levels. Needless to say, it was mentally exhausting – adding to the physical exhaustion of having commuted to London a few times this week and having spent all free moments working on our stable conversion – hence the need for ice cream and more gin than tonic in my G&T tonight.

The episode ends and rolls into another. They're addictively short. This feels like necessary escapism.

"We should try and get on top of all the safety stuff before Jo comes round again," Clare says, putting down the ice cream tub and reaching for a notebook on the coffee table, "so we're not caught off guard again."

We're slowly working through a list of changes the safety inspector has asked us to make to our home. She came round last month and, thankfully, was more reasonable in her assessment than Stewart, deeming our property an appropriate venue for children if we made a few changes – though by 'a few changes' we're talking an extensive list. We've not been very systematic in our execution of the list, much to my shame. Jo keeps checking on our progress, so we make hurried attempts at botched measures prior to her visits.

Having been instructed to move all our alcohol from a low shelf in the kitchen to somewhere secure, we ended up bunging it all in our upstairs ensuite shower moments before Jo's visit last week, away from her prying eyes. Despite this being a temporary measure, the alcohol is still waiting to find its 'forever home' (although the gin has secured its own designated spot behind the cereals in the larder, making it conveniently accessible for my nightly G&T routine).

"We still need to order some of those safety things for the cupboard doors in the kitchen," Clare says, running her finger down the list. "It feels odd toddler-proofing our house. What if we get matched with an older child who is very capable of getting a bowl out of the cupboard without smashing it?"

Or what if we decided in a few weeks that we don't actually want to do this? I think, deciding it's not the moment to say this out loud.

"And we need to get rid of the knife block," I add. At the time we'd asked the safety inspector why on earth we needed to get rid of it, laughing a little at yet another ridiculous request, only to be told that we needed to have knives in a secure location to prevent a child getting hold of one and threatening us with it. We stopped laughing and added 'remove knife block' to our list.

Clare is flapping around plumping cushions – a weekly ritual prior to Jo's arrival. I doubt voluptuous soft furnishings will distract from the fact that Jo is going to experience zero resistance when she tries opening our kitchen cupboards (child locks yet to be purchased). But I leave her to it and cut some chunks of cheese for Coben and Deaver who are weaving round my ankles in a pool of early-summer sunlight that reveals the dust in the air.

I'm looking forward to seeing Jo. Despite the intensity of her visits, I enjoy them. We're becoming increasingly fond of her. The doorbell chimes. Jo is nothing but punctual. It suits her.

I offer her, "the usual?" to which she says, "Thank you, Jeremy," while settling herself down in her favourite spot and arranging all her paperwork, some of which is slipping from a file and cascading onto the carpet. She seems to have accidently matched herself with our living room today; her pink, flowery shirt an extension of our curtains, her brown knee-length skirt blending with the couch. It's hard to determine how old she is; she's clearly been doing this a long time and she made a brief, uncharacteristic reference to a grandchild last week (no more information offered, despite Clare's gentle probing), so perhaps she's in her late 50s?

"I have another book recommendation for you!" Jo projects her voice so I can hear her as I head into the kitchen. Jo and I have bonded over books and coffee. She seems to enjoy my enthusiasm for her reading list. "It's about one couple's experience of adopting two children who experienced trauma in their early life. It's a bit different – more immersive, less textbook. You might enjoy it too, Clare," she adds. Clare's been eager about the prospect of reading lots, but a little less thorough perhaps.

I make Jo her strong coffee with a dash of milk, listening to Clare chat away about how lovely the warmer weather is and how we've been enjoying working on the garden – slipping in that we're soon to erect the long-awaited chicken wire – and asking Jo how her trip to London was (she seldom reveals such details, but this trip required her to rearrange our session this week). Jo 'mmm's' along politely, offering little in return and responding with a mere, "It was very helpful, thank you," in response to Clare's question about London. She's warm, but aloof, which exasperates Clare, who is uncomfortable with the fact that Jo knows everything about her, while she knows next to nothing about Jo.

"I've got something to show you," Jo says, once we're all settled in the living room. She likes to keep things to the point. She hands us a flyer. It's entitled 'Fostering for Adoption' and has a logo saying 'Coram' in the corner.

"Fostering for Adoption, or foster to adopt, is a new initiative that has been successfully piloted in London by a children's charity called Coram," she explains, pointing to an explanation in the flyer:

I scan the text: *Fostering for Adoption allows those who want to adopt children to foster them while they are waiting for the court to decide if adoption is the right plan for the child. This would provide continuity of care for the child, as they would not have to be placed with temporary foster carers.*

"So with Fostering for Adoption, when a baby is taken into care at birth they are placed straight with their prospective adoptive parents, who foster them while a decision is made by the court as to where they should be placed long term," Jo elaborates. "Sometimes, the baby or child returns to their birth parents, or is adopted by someone in the extended birth family; on other occasions an adoption order is granted and the child stays with the couple they've been fostered by.

"I think it's an excellent initiative," she continues. "It means that the carers take on the risk, not the child. Either the child experiences continuity of care and remains with the same people who have been fostering them from the start – which is often from the moment they're discharged from hospital – or they return to their birth parents. Either way the child wins.

"And all the while the child has a secure foundation for attachments to take place, avoiding the trauma and damage that can happen when moving around foster carers. It means the child can have a robust sense of belonging right from the start and the bonding process for adoptive parents can start sooner." Jo's leaning forward, gesturing with her hands. Animated and clearly passionate about this approach.

"I'd love to try this here in Somerset. You two would be excellent guinea pigs."

Never have I seen Clare so enthusiastic about being called a guinea pig. I could tell she was hooked from the word 'baby'. We exchange looks.

"As I've said, there are risks for the prospective adoptive parent," she cautions, noting the look of glee on Clare's face, "as there is always a possibility that the court could rule in favour of the child returning to their birth parent. There is no guarantee that the child will eventually be adopted. But if they *are* the benefits for the adoptive parents are endless; knowing the child from a very young age and able to bond and form a secure attachment earlier."

"Just to clarify," Clare says, "we're talking about babies? As in, babies who are going straight into care?"

"Not exclusively," Jo clarifies, with a note of caution, "but yes, this is a rare adoption approach which allows prospective adopters to be involved in a child's life from weeks old."

I'm hooked, but full of questions, many of which I know will fully form once Jo has left. We continue to discuss the benefits for the child and the risks for those hoping to adopt them. We don't talk about my reservations about being guinea pigs, and whether social services have thought through how this would be rolled out.

"Have a think and let me know," Jo concludes, "there's no rush". I can tell Clare is biting her tongue – I'm pretty sure she'd commit us to the next baby born if she could.

"Let's get back to business," Jo continues, steering us to the PAR questions – today, we're being gently assessed on how we deal with conflict in our relationship among other things. But the next hour is a struggle, I can tell Clare is distracted. When Jo asks what annoys her about me she gives a vague, predictable response, "oh, tricky... I guess when he puts his dirty clothes *next* to the wash bin rather than *in* it. And he seems to suffer from some sort of short-term memory defect, which is pretty irritating." I match her ambiguity with, "her strange mouse-like sneezes that go on forever. It's so infuriating."

Towards the end, Jo hands us a few printouts of children waiting to be adopted – "through traditional adoption methods," she clarifies, "Not through Fostering for Adoption, which would typically be for babies or very young children, as I've said". We've seen a few of these 'catalogues', for want of a better word; they make both Clare and me feel deeply uncomfortable... the thought of choosing a child based off a picture and a brief summary feels absurd. Jo mainly shows us these for reference – a learning exercise in being able to read between the lines, the adoption equivalent of interpreting an estate agent's description: 'needs decorating' equals 'complete disaster'; 'some emotional needs' equals 'major anger management issues'.

I look down at the sheet. This feels too much for today, I'm ready for Jo to go. But I follow along as she directs our attention to the top left, a picture of two siblings, "five and three" she says, "you said you might be interested in a sibling group?"

We are; the thought of becoming a family of four or five instantaneously feels exciting. At least I think it does. "What questions would you have about this sibling group, for example?" she asks.

Clare says nothing. My brain is out of action.

After a painful five minutes of Jo drawing answers out of us like blood from a stone, she checks her watch and wraps things up; ending on a suitably awkward note with her final question: "Just want to check that you guys are using contraception? Remember you *must* be using contraception when going through the adoption process."

I usher Jo to the door, assuring her that we have contraception. This is true, I don't want to lie. But have we used said contraception? Well no. After nearly ten years of trying, I don't think we're going to accidently have a baby at this point. And for some reason, Clare's stopped getting pregnant – the final round of IVF, nearly two years ago, being the last time. The theory is that she has a low egg count now, so the chance of a pregnancy, especially a successful one, feels slim if not impossible.

Summer and autumn pass and we're into early November before we know it. Amidst all the uncertainties we feel the need to escape. Goa, India has long been on my bucket list. I'm hoping that a big adventure will serve as a diversion as we anticipate facing our Adoption Panel in a few weeks. We're confident we'll be approved to adopt but feel nervous either way. What if we don't get approved? What if we *do?*

We completed our PAR in October and, following much discussion, officially agreed to be social services Fostering for Adoption guinea pigs in Somerset; providing we are approved by the panel, and providing the powers that be in social services agree it's worth trialling Fostering for Adoption in the area. There are a lot of 'ifs' that need to align, but we're convinced by the benefits of this approach; that *we* should be the ones to shoulder the risks and uncertainties, not the child.

If we're honest, we're also gripped by the possibility of being able to nurture a baby from birth. We have been warned that this won't be without complications – the child may well have been exposed to harmful substances while in the womb and there could be significant health issues that are not evident at birth. But given everything we've learnt about attachment and the impacts of early abuse and neglect, we're eager to know a child as early in their life as possible.

Last month we attended a three-day parenting course – a prerequisite to completing the application process – and attachment was a reoccurring theme, hammering home the impact on a child who spends time moving between foster homes, frequently experiencing severed attachments. It was an intense few days, but ultimately reassuring. On day one of the course there were eight of us – four couples. By day two there were six. It felt like we were being slowly picked off by an assassin; a sequence of events designed, in part, to see if we can hack even thinking about the worst-case scenario, let alone living through it. It's been nine months since we started exploring adoption and we're still here, yet to be knocked out. Maybe this is all the confirmation we need that we're doing the right thing.

These parenting courses only run a few times a year, and as fate would have it, we had already booked holiday that week in an attempt to finish renovating the stables behind the house into offices. It's frequent small instances like this, conveniently coincidental, that make us wonder if God is in this adoption idea (and perhaps less fussed about the stable renovation – with all recent attempts at progress on the project being usurped).

Clare and I have prayed at points over the last few months; both feeling the urge to metaphorically get on our knees and invite God into the uncertainty and unknown, or recognise that he's already there, somewhere, present amidst the unknown, comfortable in uncertainty. Prayer has felt hard in recent years – petitions seemingly falling on deaf ears – but we both still feel compelled to lay our hopes and fears before God and are surprised, afresh, at how anxiety can be exchanged for peace. We haven't felt any clear divine direction as to whether we should go ahead with adoption or not, so we've pressed on, and things seem to be working out. Perhaps God is in the 'working out', gently nudging us forward.

We're thirty minutes into the three hour journey to the airport (traffic permitting) and I'm beginning to wonder what it will take to distract Clare. She's talking about Fostering for Adoption again, hypothesising about what might happen after our matching panel and whether we'll have a baby in a few months' time, and what that baby might be like and what a great dad I'll be. It's a fairly repetitive monologue. I nod along, diverting the conversation to holiday plans, only to have Clare expertly loop us back round to adoption through some tenuous link in the conversation. If the vibrancy of Goa can't distract Clare for the next few weeks, I don't know what will.

There's no queue for check-in and baggage drop-off when we arrive – a relief as we're definitely cutting things fine – and we make a dash for security. Clare's phone rings. "Just ignore it," I say, "we've not got time."

"But it's Jo," she says, breaking into a trot – her legs are significantly shorter than mine and she's struggling to keep up. We always pick up to Jo. Clare puts her on speaker.

"I hope I've caught you at a good moment?" Jo says after brief 'hellos'. Well no, but Clare says, "yes, of course". I roll my eyes at her.

"I just wanted to keep you in the loop. There is a woman known to social services who is pregnant and due to give birth at some point around Christmas. We think that Fostering for Adoption would be really beneficial for this child." We slow down, forgetting the immediate urgency.

"So, this could be the one?" Clare says, to clarify. "For us?"

"There are a lot of unknowns at this stage," Jo warns. "You still need to be approved as adopters, and I'm still discussing the details and various approvals of Fostering for Adoption with social services. It's all up in the air. But, yes, there is a chance this could be the one for you."

I ask Jo if she can tell us any more, but as expected she says, "no, not at this stage. But I did want to let you know what we're considering." We thank her and she hangs up.

Over the next few weeks we think about this unborn baby; while riding elephants, jumping on and off moving trains, careering around Panaji in tuk-tuks and cruising down the Mandovi river in an ornate wooden houseboat. This child consumes our thoughts, our conversations, our prayers. Until now everything has been theoretical. Until now we've somewhat sat on the fence. But now we're talking about a real situation, a real child, something has shifted.

We wonder what he or she will be called, and turn over the baby names we love again; William, like my father and grandfather; Christabella or Bella after Clare's mum. I like to think of myself as a considered, measured person, not inclined to being emotionally unrestrained, but I can practically feel the swelling of uncontrollable emotional investment. The prospect of becoming parents feels more tangible; tantalisingly close.

On arriving home we have a few days to prepare for our Adoption Panel; by which I mean, recover from our over-stimulating holiday, get some work done and anxiously wait. Clare goes to town on the Christmas decorations in an attempt to distract herself.

The panel is held at County Hall; a beautiful, neo-Georgian style building, curving inward like a row of crescent houses. The grandeur ups the nerves; the black and white checked marble floor giving the impression of being in a giant game of chess, our fate in the balance. Unexpectedly, I find myself thinking back to Clare's flippant, rhetorical question all those years ago when we decided we wanted to start a family, 'How hard can it be?' she'd said. Flaming hard, it turns out.

Twenty minutes before we go in we're given some questions to consider. They're all based off our PAR; one is about our church involvement (I think they're trying to find out if we would indoctrinate a child in our care), another is about our motivation to adopt. I act composed and professional as we discuss our answers, with Jo interjecting advice every now and again.

Under the surface I'm uneasy. This is the strangest test I've ever undertaken – being judged on my suitability to be a father. This is our final bid to become parents. My feeling of unease grows as our twenty minutes of prep time extends to forty. The couple who went in before us had to wait a long time as their application and answers were deliberated by the panel. Their social worker has just appeared with the verdict; I can't hear what's being said, but it's clear from the look on their faces that they've not been successful.

There are nine people gathered in the room when we enter. We're introduced to two social workers, a medical advisor, four independent members who have personal experiences of adoption, and a panel chair and secretary. We sit before them, interview style, with the reassuring presence of Jo alongside us.

My confidence builds as we answer the questions articulately and with ease. When asked about church we assure the panel that we plan to nurture a child to think openly and critically about life and faith, offering our worldview while providing space for them to form their own perspectives. They nod contentedly in response, and move on to questioning us about our support network and our experience of the assessment process.

One of the social workers begins quizzing Jo about Fostering for Adoption, they seem intrigued and invested, nudging the proceedings momentarily off-piste and reminding us how novel this new adoption approach is to the experts as well as us, until the chair firmly brings us back on track. We're asked to leave the room while they deliberate our future.

We wait for about ten minutes, predominantly in silence – unusual for Clare – until the chair of the panel emerges. She's beaming.

"You're unanimously approved!" she announces with relish. The relief! We all exchange hugs and I thank Jo for her guidance and support, echoed enthusiastically by Clare.

I wait as Clare adorns herself with jumper, coat and scarf and picks up various items and bits of paperwork she's acquired from somewhere. Exiting places would be infinitely quicker if she just used the bag I bought for her last Christmas – she's got so many bags, why doesn't she use them? I consider making this point, but decide it's probably not the right time and instead turn to Jo to ask what happens next.

Her answer is not unexpected. We wait. She will be in touch soon. It feels anti-climactic. We leave – the majestic backdrop of County Hall behind us, the chaos of the one-way system in front – and head back into normal life.

We meet my parents for Mum's birthday lunch. They seem keen to celebrate us being approved as adopters as much – if not more – than Mum's birthday, their delight and excitement for us dominating the conversation. We try not to get too caught up in their enthusiasm, knowing we need to monitor our expectations and get back into the flow of daily life. We could be waiting a while, we need to pace ourselves.

For the next few days, I'm working in London and I distract myself as much as possible, to the point where the thought of a bit of normality for a while feels reasonable and possibly quite refreshing. "Maybe we need a bit of time to take a breath," Clare writes in a message while I'm away. I agree. The waiting could be ok.

And then, the next morning, I get the call that pierces through my briefly re-established normality and changes the trajectory of everything.

"Wilson! Get on a train and come home, NOW!" Clare practically screams down the phone, taking bossy to another level. Before I get a chance to ask why, she explains that Jo has called.

"The baby she told us about before we left for Goa – you know, *the* baby – was born prematurely a few weeks ago," Clare says, breathy with excitement. "A boy! Jo has been waiting to finalise a few things – something about paperwork or something like that – before letting us know. She's asked if we want to come to County Hall *tomorrow* to chat to her more and meet the baby's social worker!"

She takes a breath and I step outside the office, light-headed with sudden anticipation. I ask Clare lots of questions, most of which she doesn't know the answers to.

"I wasn't really listening properly," she admits. Right, that's helpful. "But she did say something about him being born with that condition where they've been exposed to drug abuse in the womb."

"Neonatal abstinence syndrome." I fill in her blank. They talked about this in one of the courses we went on.

"Yes, that. And that he's in the neonatal intensive care unit."

"Do you remember what time Jo said we should be there tomorrow?" Please say she's remembered this important detail.

"Nine am... No wait... No yes, nine am. It was definitely nine am." She doesn't sound very definite, but at least it's early, so we can wait around if she's misremembered.

"I'll be on the next train." I hang up, my mind racing, caught in a momentary trance-like state before snapping into action. I need to get home.

CHAPTER 8 – The villain

Clare

"Can everyone look at the camera."

It's an instruction, not a question. I don't want to look at the camera. Everything about this moment is bizarre and unbearably awkward. What the hell is going on and *who* are these people?! I thought we were meeting with Jo and the baby's social worker. *Are we in the right room?*

I look away from the camera lens and glance at the door. I hate having my photograph taken; a loathing now exacerbated by the fact that I have no idea what's going on and feel very out of control.

Jeremy is standing to my right. I can tell from his posture that he's feeling as uncomfortable as I am. He's placed a gentle, reassuring hand on my back. To my left stands a woman who I've 'known' for all of about sixty seconds. I don't know it yet, but she's about to become a significant part of my life, hence why we're posing for this 'happy family' picture.

The first thing I noticed when I was ushered into this small, non-descript room in County Hall a few moments ago was her ginger hair; thin and wiry, like her figure. I usually feel an instant kinship with gingers and I'm not intentionally withholding my affinity in this instance, but *this* ginger is extremely angry about something and I'm subconsciously bracing against her aggression.

She glanced in our direction when we walked in, but immediately returned to ranting to a red-faced woman who looked somewhat official – maybe a social worker?

"You're fuckin' kiddin' me!" the ginger one was yelling. "You're not fuckin' takin' Sienna away!"

"I'm afraid you can't ignore the court order, Stacey. There's nothing I can do about it now," the official one had said, almost apologetically.

"*Fuck* your court orders! I'm not fuckin' goin'! No fuckin' way. And I'm not givin' 'im, up either..." she'd taken a deep breath before shouting, "Fuck you all!"

Jeremy had paused, eyebrows raised, wincing slightly, looking back at the door with a 'should we be in here?!' quizzical expression on his face. It didn't sound like a conversation we should be privy to. But before we could escape, a man with a camera had jumped in and herded us together for a picture, without any explanation and with such command that we found ourselves falling into place and smiling at the camera without question. I guess he was eager to do his job and get out of there as fast as possible.

I'm very conscious of the angry ginger stood next to me as we pose for the camera. She smells of cigarette smoke and her breathing is fast and heavy. She's swearing profusely under her breath. The way she holds herself suggests she's uncomfortable in her body. I wonder if she's smiling at the camera. I imagine not. I am. Though I'm not sure why.

Behind me, slightly to the left, stands a man. I've not had a chance to take him in yet, other than he's tall, like Jeremy, and he has a receding hairline and prominent nose. His eyes are dark and sunken; he looks tired. So far he's been quiet. The photographer lowers his camera and we immediately disperse, resuming some much-needed personal space.

"Er, I'm Jeremy," says Jeremy, extending a hand to the tall man, attempting to claw back some order to the proceedings. Whatever these proceedings are! I'm thoroughly confused. Assuming we're in the right room – Jo has now appeared behind us and doesn't seem phased by the scene, though perhaps a tad exasperated – I wonder whether this couple could be the baby's birth parents? But no one has said this yet and I wasn't expecting to meet them today. I thought we were just coming in for a quick chat with Jo and the baby's social worker to find out more.

"Yes, introductions!" Jo interrupts, before the tall man has a chance to reply. Phew. Thank God for Jo.

"This is Craig and Stacey, Graydon's birth parents. And Jeremy and Clare, the foster parents," she says gesturing around the room with her folder. "And Jade, Graydon's social worker."

"Hello!" Jade says too cheerfully, clearly still stressed out by Stacey's verbal barrage moments before.

Graydon. I turn this name over in my mind as if examining it from different angles, trying to like it. I don't. But I'm thinking of *him* again, this baby, and a feeling that I can't name rises in my body; it's excitement, anticipation, overwhelm, fear all rolled into one. I'm on the threshold, but also terrified this all might slip through my fingers.

"Just a little bit of paperwork to complete," Jo interrupts my thoughts with the drudge of yet another form.

I roll my eyes, playfully. "We're going to drown in all your paperwork one day, Jo!"

I'm addressing Jo but I'm looking at Stacey. I don't quite know why I'm saying this. I can feel Jeremy looking at me – it's likely to be a 'not the moment, Clare' sort of look. But it all feels so tense and stressful; I don't feel safe in this sort of environment and want to lighten the mood (for my own sake perhaps, as no one else seems particularly bothered).

I think I'm trying to throw a line to Stacey, hoping she may look at me and smile, just for a moment. I'm conscious I'm the woman taking her son away. What a role to be playing... to her I must be the villain. The thought of having to play that role in someone else's story makes me feel a bit sick.

She doesn't look up.

I open my mouth to say something else, think better of it, and get on with the form asking me yet again for some basic details that social services must surely know by heart now, they've asked me so many times.

"You driving down, Jo?" Jade asks. Down where? I wonder. I'm still confused and waiting for the promised 'chat' to commence – I'm desperate to find out more about Graydon.

Jo nods, not looking up from the form she's just been handed by Craig, which she's squinting at intently, clearly trying to decipher.

"Yes, we'll head down to the hospital to meet Graydon now," she says to me and Jeremy, returning to the room.

"Are you two walking?" She's looking at Craig now, while I mouth 'what?!' at Jeremy, who also has a flabbergasted look on his face. We get to *meet him?* Have we missed something?

"Yeh." Craig replies, nonchalantly.

"We'll walk too," Jeremy says casually despite the absurdity of the situation, putting down his pen, handing Jo the form and reaching for his coat.

Right. The bizarre, awkward moment lives on. Thanks Jeremy.

We leave County Hall with Stacey half saying, half shouting, "We still gotta chat 'bout Sienna!" over her shoulder at Jade, adding, *"fuckin'* social services," under her breath as she attempts to light a cigarette with trembling hands.

It's not raining, but the air feels wet and despite it being pretty mild for December, I draw my coat around myself tightly, crossing my arms in front. I can't help but wonder if this is ok – the four of us walking down the road together, unsupervised. It's not that I'm worried, just that the process has been pretty formal so far and this is anything but formal. Jo said we would be their guinea pigs and I feel like one; it's as if social services are making things up as they go along. Maybe they are.

Thankfully it's just a fifteen-minute walk down the road to the hospital. But despite this walk being Jeremy's idea, he doesn't say anything as we walk away from County Hall. It's probably a matter of seconds, but I already feel the urge to fill the moment with words. There are very few people I can actually enjoy being silent with – Jeremy, Carol, a few select friends, and of course Mum... But despite the awkward silence, and my urge to lag behind with Jeremy and regain composure, this feels like an opportunity to glean more information; we're so in the dark right now.

"We're really excited to meet Graydon," I say to Stacey.

"Yeh, 'e's well cute." She meets my eyes properly for the first time, and regardless of how indifferent and stand-off-ish she's been so far, I feel a wave of empathy for this woman that makes me want to lean in. What's happened in her life that's brought her to the point of having to give up the child she's just given birth to? It feels so unimaginable and I feel so removed from her world. But here we are, our worlds colliding.

As we walk along – this unexpected party of four – I ask her about the birth and how Graydon's doing. Jo's not told us much, only that he was born with neonatal abstinence syndrome – a condition brought on by substance abuse in the womb. So I'm surprised when Stacey gives a glowing health report and an account of the birth that makes it sound like he basically popped out with zero effort (the sort of birth story that would make Carol reel – 'if they say it was simple and pain free they're *lying*!' I hear her voice say). But I accept this story as truth (why would I not?) and feel grateful to have had the moment to 'connect' with her, if you can call it that.

"Why did you call him Graydon?" Jeremy asks from behind, as Craig and Stacey lead the way through a maze of hospital buildings. He's sticking much more to script – this is the sort of question we've been told to ask.

"We was gonna call him William," Stacey says, pausing to stub out another cigarette before leading us indoors.

"That's a *lovely* name," I say, catching Jeremy's eye.

"Yeh, Craig's grandad's name. But then he was bein' a dick so we picked Graydon instead." She looks across at Craig like there's more to this story, but says no more.

I note the signs pointing us in the direction of the neonatal intensive care unit and my heart quickens. Stacey presses the intercom and announces her arrival. She doesn't mention us. Automatic doors to the unit open ceremoniously before us and Jo and Jade are there waiting.

"Hello!" We're greeted enthusiastically again by Jade; like bosom friends. It's too much for Jeremy, who prefers subtle, appropriate greetings, but I don't mind. Her warmth has made me feel a bit more relaxed.

"Jeremy, can you come with me?" Jo asks. "Graydon's doctor is going to give you a full assessment of his health to-date, and I need you to sign a few more forms." She starts walking before he's replied, so Jeremy follows, glancing back at me for a moment.

I'm ushered into a room down the corridor. Stacey has gone in ahead and is bustling around, fussing over an incubator and making cooing noises, watched closely by the duty nurse who seems frustrated and unimpressed by her presence.

I see him. He's lying on his back, arms casually flung above his head. He's wearing a dark blue t-shirt saying 'Good Looking', little baby-blue striped trousers and tiny white socks that are too big for him. There's a rubber hand on his chest for comfort and a clear tube coming out of his nose. He's asleep, but it doesn't look like peaceful sleep; one of his hands is twitching slightly and his brow is furrowed.

I swallow. I feel like I could cry, but I don't. I stand there like a lemon, looking round the room and wondering what I should be doing. I take my coat off, suddenly noticing how hot and clammy I feel.

"Perhaps Clare would like to hold him," Jade says pointedly to Stacey. A nurse removes his intravenous line and hands him to Stacey, who fumbles a bit and places him in my arms. The nurse gestures to me to sit down, like I'm a liability and might trip over.

I cradle him and I want the world to stop so I can savour this moment. I want them all to go away and Jeremy to be here. I'm transfixed by him. I'm holding my breath. I want to draw him closer to me, kiss his forehead, rub my cheek against his and breathe deeply. I want to cradle him and study him. I want him to hear my voice. I want him to know that I was devoted to him even before I met him and that I've never felt a surge of love so strong. I sense deeply in my bones that he's mine to love.

But I feel all their eyes on me. I feel *her* eyes on me; the woman who carried him and birthed him. She's watching me intently. Loathing me.

I could not be less alone. And now the bloody photographer is back – argh! – and despite being a self-assured thirty-seven-year-old who wants to say a firm 'no!', the moment tumbles and I roll with it. Stacey draws up a chair next to me at the photographer's request and places a hand on Graydon's leg like I need help holding him. Craig comes behind us, a firm hand on my shoulder, and I smile.

"Great!" The photographer enthuses. "A lovely one for his Life Story Book." I get it, it's important for Graydon to one day know that we met, but is *this* the moment?

Then I get my wish. Jade says they need to get to court – something about Sienna again – and Stacey's expression immediately hardens as they gather their coats and leave. I'm nearly alone with him, only the quiet presence of another nurse who's just walked in. She shows me how to wrap him up tightly in a muslin, like a little pupa, to calm him and stop him from twitching.

His little body stills.

"Hello," I whisper in awe. Then I pause. I can't bring myself to call him Graydon; it seems strange... it doesn't suit him. He looks like a William, and it *was* going to be his name. Before I've taken time to dwell on it, I find myself whispering this name to him. "*William*. Hello William," I say, and it resonates. I'm aware we'll need to talk to Jo about this, and that we shouldn't change his name lightly, but I can feel that for us, from now, he'll be William.

I know there is no guarantee that he will be ours forever, but I can't, and won't, and don't believe this right now. Finally, I'm holding my child. *This* is my baby. I can't contain the feeling so I offer it up, "Father, thank you." For the first time in a long time I feel seen; like the guttural cries of my heart have been heard, that God has broken his silence and revealed that he was always listening.

"I was there when he was born," the nurse's soft voice breaks my moment, but I welcome her intrusion.

"I prayed over him in the first moments of his life." She looks at me knowingly. "I held him through those first long, hard nights when he was distressed."

Prayed? It feels like a bold thing for a medical professional to say. Had she heard my whispered prayer? I'm even more overwhelmed and moved. Tears prick the corners of my eyes. The contrast of the last hour feels so stark; the awkwardness of meeting Stacey and Craig compared to *this* moment which couldn't feel more right. I have an overwhelming sense that there is nowhere else I'm meant to be than with this little boy. I'm all in.

Jeremy walks in and I note afresh how calm and reassured I feel, simply by his presence. He doesn't need to say anything. I'm so glad he's here.

His eyes are on William – and I pass him over as Jeremy sits down. "Your son," I whisper.

Nothing could have prepared me for this moment; the sense of completeness. Tomorrow is my birthday. I think of all the times I asked Jeremy for a baby for my birthday. I am so ready.

A few days later and we're in the depths of Mothercare.

There are lots of things I've looked forward to about becoming a mum; one thing is the *stuff*. Everyone complains about it – all the things you have to get for a tiny human – but I'm thrilled at the prospect of finally being able to bring all the baby paraphernalia into our house. And I intend to get myself a new bag for all my baby bits and bobs. You can't have too many bags.

I'm trying to revel in this longed-for shopping experience but it's been an emotional week with a lot to process and I'm feeling a bit foggy.

We've seen William every day; I find it so hard leaving him. He's often unsettled when I put him down and I ache looking at him there; alone in his glass box with only the rubber hand for comfort. I wish I could stay with him, but am told I can't. It feels like a mini trauma leaving him there every day, so poorly and abandoned.

We spent the whole day with him on my birthday – a dream come true in every respect, until I had to put him down and walk away. We drove straight to Jeremy's parents' house for my birthday dinner, and my agony at leaving him was tempered by surprise Christmas wreath making organised by Pat, my ever-attentive mother-in-law; the therapeutic repetitive motion of weaving ivy around willow branches in safe company helping me regain composure.

We told them about meeting William, but waited until yesterday – having just received confirmation from Jo that he would be discharged into our care in a few days' time – before revealing that we would be bringing him home.

We savoured this moment, sitting around the table at Rachel and David's having a Sunday roast, with Jeremy expertly waiting for a lull in the conversation and then casually asking if there would be room for one more small person at the table on Christmas day – the baby reveal we (and they) had been waiting nine years for! There was an eruption of noise and I basked in the sheer elation of shared joy. They've embraced him as their own already. William is part of the family.

Since that first precious encounter with William we've been weaving our daily hospital visits around Stacey, so we're not there at the same time. The other woman... I have to share my baby.

A bit of me loathes her – is that too strong? I hold him tight as he twitches; his little body writhing from the discomfort and distress of withdrawing from heroin. His cry is incessant. He's hard to calm, like he can't find peace. He's done nothing to deserve this start in life. How could she inflict this on him? It feels so inhumane. But there, amidst my loathing, is a profound sadness for her too. I gather him in as she is being disentangled. My gain is her loss. Tonight we get to stay overnight in the hospital with him and then *we*, not she, will bring him home. She walks away empty-handed.

Life is downright weird at the moment. It's a lot to process. Definitely too much to be thinking about while I stand here feeling bemused in the bottles and teats aisle of Mothercare. There are so many. How on earth should we know which to choose?

Jeremy makes some joke about the weird knobbly-looking NUK teats resembling mine, making them the obvious choice, and I stifle a laugh and give him a thump as a store assistant approaches. She is looking at me wondering why I don't look pregnant and why I'm there. Jeremy later says this isn't true, but it's definitely the expression I saw – you can tell a lot from the positioning of someone's eyebrows. I add 'imposter syndrome' to the list of complex emotions I'm currently battling with.

I give a garbled explanation of our situation and feel reassured by how helpful and understanding she is – although I'm still convinced she's looking at me like I don't really belong. We part with an alarming amount of money and pile all the equipment in the boot of our car. I see Jeremy carefully tuck away the receipts in his wallet.

Jo has told us to keep hold of them, just in case everything falls through. She keeps reminding us that it's all very precarious. I have to resist the urge to grab them and rip them into tiny pieces.

This stuff is never going back.

It's three am and we've been holding William all night. We're taking it in turns so one of us can rest, but we've both got too much adrenaline pumping through our veins to sleep and, besides, it feels like a two-person job. How I'll ever manage nappy changes on my own I have no idea – there's been wee everywhere and a lot of hushed cries of "Jeremy, more wet wipes! Now!"

The nurses have been so patient and kind. They've given us our own room in the old part of the ward, away from the swanky new neonatal intensive care unit (NICU) development. It feels like going back into the 1960s. But, despite the dated interior, I'm grateful for the space. We've been shown how to feed him, wash him and change his nappy. It's not rocket science, but at three in the morning it seems to be requiring all my attention. I keep hoping I'll see her again – the nurse who was there when he was born – but I haven't. I'm not sure what I think about angels, but if they're real she certainly fits the bill.

William is three and a half weeks old, but he's still so poorly. He trembles and sneezes constantly; cries and startles when we put him down. From what the nurses have said, his first few days were touch and go – the worst case of neonatal abstinence syndrome they'd ever seen. "I really didn't think he'd make it," one of them told us. It makes me want to hold him closer. He doesn't want to be put down and I don't want to put him down. I feel fiercely protective.

The vibes among the nurses towards Stacey are pretty negative, with one candidly sharing what a liability she has been – even stealing some of William's Oramorph (oral morphine) on one occasion, the drug they're giving him to help with his withdrawal. What?! He suffers more so she can get a mini fix?! It's mind-boggling and infuriating.

I feel waves of indignation but at the same time physically ache for her, and pity the grief that's been thrust upon her. The day we met her – when she was raging at Jade – she'd just found out that her daughter, Sienna, was being placed for adoption on the same day that her newborn son was also being taken into care. No wonder she was practically kicking and screaming – her children were being taken away.

I notice Jeremy has dozed off, slumped in an upright chair in the corner of the room. He stirs five minutes later in response to William's wails, flinging himself into action before he's properly come round. We snatch moments of fretful sleep here and there until the morning rounds. A nurse makes various checks and then talks us through how to give Oramorph to William when we get home.

He's been getting the drug through an intravenous line until now, although I thought he'd been weaned off a few days ago. "Ah yes, you're right," the nurse confirms, "but he was really unsettled the night before last so the nurse on duty gave him some to calm him.

So, we're prescribing you a small dose in case he needs help with his withdrawal over the next few days. Doctor's advice is to wean him off it as soon as possible though," she adds. I'm nodding along but pretty convinced we'll be taking the doctor's advice to wean him and won't be giving him any Oramorph. We know that going cold turkey will be hard for him and for us, but it will happen at some point and we're prepared to hold him every second through it. The thought of continuing to give him such a strong drug feels wrong.

Jo arrives with a Tesco bag of baby clothes from Stacey. We haven't seen Stacey since that first day. She's been there in my mind, but I've also tried to forget about her, preferring to soak up our little family of three without dwelling too much on the complications. As I look through the bag of clothes Jo points out a particular outfit that Stacey would like me to dress William in as we take him home from hospital today. The clothes still have British Heart Foundation tags on them, suggesting they've been grabbed from the charity shop round the corner. These are the clothes I'm meant to dress him in from now on. In the eyes of the law I am merely his minder; his temporary foster carer. In the eyes of the law he is still ultimately hers, and she can tell me what she does and doesn't want him dressed in.

I don't want him in these clothes.

But, of course, I say nothing and nod along as Jo reminds me that we'll start contact sessions on Thursday – two days from now – "so Stacey and Graydon can have some time together and continue to develop a bond," she explains. His name's not Graydon, I think, as Jo goes on to tell me that we should bring him to contact dressed in the clothes Stacey has provided. I'm not being territorial – I don't think I am anyway – if anything, I feel so broken for Stacey right now. But his name's not Graydon and he's not wearing these clothes. And he's about to come home with us, forever. I know I'm not meant to think like this, and if I said this out loud right now Jo would caution me, but how can I be expected to feel anything else?

Jeremy packs up our stuff, which is strewn across the room like we've been living here for a week, while I start changing William into the outfit Stacey has chosen. It smells of smoke, so I make a subtle switch and slip him into a white baby grow instead, quickly putting the blue snowsuit Pat and Bill bought for him over the top before Jo notices. I congratulate myself for being smooth (not something I'm often, if ever, described as) and tuck Stacey's choice outfit into the Tesco bag with the other clothes, planning to wash them in time for our first contact session. I only feel a tiny bit sneaky. I can't be expected to keep him in clothes that smell of smoke.

Jo asks if we've got the prescribed Oramorph and I make a joke about it being Christmas and William going cold turkey. The joke falls flat, but I notice the sides of Jeremy's mouth twitching.

"We've got the Oramorph, yes," I add hastily in a more serious tone, attempting to justify my joke, "but the doctor has recommended that we wean him off it as soon as possible." Jo nods. There's a moment of silence. Only I seem to find it awkward.

"I gather we need to take this milk home?" I raise my eyebrows, gesturing to a bag that contains Stacey's drug-infused breastmilk.

"Ah yes," Jo says. "Put it in the freezer as soon as you get home. Don't use it, of course – I know you know that," she adds as Jeremy and I chorus "no, no, of course not". "But it could be helpful to use in the court case, so it's worth hanging on to," she explains. I'm not sure how I feel about Stacey's druggy milk hanging out next to my beloved mint choc chip ice cream, or why our freezer needs to be used to store evidence, but I don't have the energy to ask so pack it next to the unwanted clothes.

A nurse escorts us out the hospital, carrying William in the car seat we bought from Mothercare the other day. "This is what it's like in films," I say to Jeremy as we trot along behind with Jo, our ever-present chaperone. It feels so surreal and we're engulfed with a silent contentment as we drive home with William in the back, and then unload everything into the dining room, William nestled in my arms.

Jo is moments behind us, bustling in and then "nipping to the loo."

"The lock on this toilet door should be higher up," she says as she comes out, gesturing back at the bathroom. "So he doesn't accidently lock himself in."

Jeremy and I look at each other and then at William, "I guess we don't need to worry about that for a little while then," Jeremy says smiling. I laugh. This scenario is meant to be funny, right? But the look on Jo's face suggests otherwise. We know that look; it's kind, it's understanding, but it also says 'I have a job to do and boxes that need to be ticked, so crack on'.

Minutes later Jeremy's toolbox is out and, satisfied, Jo smiles and takes her leave, urging us to call if we need anything. Despite how ridiculous this moment feels – ticking boxes just for the sake of it before we've even had a chance to take our coats off – I don't want her to leave. She's a reassuring presence, and however much I've longed for this moment it now feels quite strange, almost a little frightening, for it to be just the three of us.

But I smile and say goodbye. And now I'm standing here, holding this tiny boy who is mine – but I'm told is not mine – with the lights of the Christmas tree in the background, watching Jeremy with his screwdriver and wondering what on earth happens next.

CHAPTER 9 – A village

Clare

Most people have nine months to prepare for a baby arriving. We had four days.

You could say we had been preparing for years, ever since the baby proposal at the top of the Eiffel Tower. How could I possibly not be ready for this? But despite all those years of hoping and praying, these first five weeks of having William have been a disorienting whirlwind. Throughout the application process to become adoptive parents we've been told – with repeated conviction – that it can take *years*... so we'd prepared ourselves that it would take *years* and allowed ourselves *years* to get our heads around actually becoming adopters.

But here we are already. Fully immersed. And naturally, I'm so thankful – I'm so done with the agonising wait, and so ready for motherhood to start – but I'm also paddling frantically under the surface. I could not be more ready... but I'm not. Does that make sense? My life is a dichotomy.

It can be hard to get out and about with William some days – between his three-hourly feeds and naps he spends most of the time crying. It's not as incessant as the early days, but even at two months old he's still experiencing withdrawal from the drugs he was exposed to in the womb, and easily becomes distressed. Sounds, smells and bright lights trigger him – I've stopped wearing perfume; Jeremy uses less spice when he's cooking; we only play quiet, calming music.

We try to mute his surroundings wherever possible, which has been a tad tricky over the Christmas period, but despite the risk of overstimulation and the exhaustion I feel when I even thinking about leaving the house for something I don't *have* to do, Jo is encouraging me to go to some baby groups. She says that I need to find my 'village'.

So I'm sat in the local village hall with a load of other mums and babies – no dads, I note.

An older lady comes over and asks if I'd like a tea or coffee... I don't. "Water please," I say, already feeling like an outsider for not being fond of a hot beverage. And as if to reinforce the point, a mum sat on the floor a few meters away, supporting a chubby-legged 10-month-ish-old says, "Wow, I don't know how I'd function without coffee."

I laugh. "I'm addicted to diet coke if that counts."

She doesn't say anything. Maybe it doesn't.

"How old's your little one?" I ask. No one's talked to me since I came in – I guess they all know each other already – so I'm keen to keep the conversation going with my new caffeine-loving acquaintance. I've daydreamed about the mum-friend experience; this is my moment.

"She's six months on Tuesday."

Sheesh she's big, I think. William was only five pounds five ounces when he was born. I forget how small he is. This baby definitely looks bigger than six months.

"How about yours?" she asks politely.

Yours. I like that. He *is* mine. I spend most of my time with social services who call him Graydon and like to constantly remind me that he's not mine, so I'm enjoying the assumption she's made.

"About two months," I say. If I'm honest, I've lost count. Does that make me a bad mum?

"Awww, still so little," my friend says (can we call her that yet?). "Are you recovering ok?"

"Oh, from his birth? I didn't really feel much!" I say. Because I didn't – we were thousands of miles away riding elephants in Goa when he was born. I don't want to lie, but I also don't feel ready to divulge my whole story to this stranger (she's still a stranger I've decided). As I say these words I think of Stacey's comments about birth, which feel uncomfortably similar.

I squirm internally. This was clearly the wrong thing to say. My stranger-friend thins her lips and raises her eyebrows, "Oh. Right!" she says, looking sideways at a woman sat next to her and then busying herself with subtly getting her boob out from under multiple layers.

She turns the conversation to weaning and I'm quickly forgotten because I have nothing to contribute. I haven't even thought about weaning. To be honest, I haven't even thought about tomorrow. Life feels both painfully slow and hectic. I can't keep track.

William's stirring. I look at my watch – ten fifty-five, he's nearly due a feed. We have to follow certain advice – or rather, rules! – while we're in the fostering phase, including following a specific feeding schedule. I would like to be more responsive to him, hone my instincts and tap into his natural rhythms, but I don't feel free or empowered to do this. I have to do exactly what social services tell me, or exactly what Stacey tells them she'd like me to do, even what formula milk she wants me to use. I guess there's no point even thinking about weaning, I'll have to do exactly what I'm told anyway. I have no choice in the matter. And I have to meticulously document everything in his days – even when he poos and when I change his nappies – to relay to social services. I'd feel bad if I fabricated this, but I find it all so restrictive and time-consuming.

I get a bottle out, give it a shake and get him settled. I can hear Jo

and the health visitor's voices in my head, "Clare, that should be freshly prepared." But how can I stick to the book and give him a fresh bottle whilst also getting out and about to discover my 'village', as instructed? The breastfeeding mum looks at me with a 'two months old and already on a bottle' look of horror. Jeremy would say I'm imagining things. I guess it's entirely possible that I'm going mad. I'm knackered.

Last night was a particularly bad one. William was hard to settle and we couldn't figure out why. Sometimes he feels like such a mystery. We feed him every three hours like clockwork, as we've been told to, but it's not like we get much of a chance to sleep in between. He takes up to an hour to feed, and then we often spend an hour settling him afterwards, swaddling him and gently rocking. If we're lucky we can put him down and keep a hand on him while one or both of us get an hour of sleep. I was horrified by the rubber hand in the hospital, but now I want one. We tried placing a beanbag snake across him, but it's not so effective.

William is starting to twist in my arms so I throw a muslin over my shoulder and hold him upright in case he needs to burp. He does, and I congratulate myself for my motherly intuition and find myself glancing around for approval. No one's looking – of course they're not, it's just a burp, not a feat deserving applause.

As I sit there, gently patting William on the back, it dawns on me. Tomorrow is contact. I groan internally. Contact... where I get to go to a random location revealed by social services the day before, just like an exciting secret club (except there's nothing exciting about it at all). And hand William over to a random person (a supervisor, who is apparently not random at all, but I'm yet to see the same person twice and I've been going three times a week for the last five weeks). And then I get the pleasure of watching him disappear into a room with said random supervisor and Stacey for a few hours. There's no other way I'd rather spend a morning.

Our first contact was the worst, and the weirdest. From what I understand these contact sessions are meant to take place in a children's centre, but with none available I was told to go to the Angel shopping centre café. I'd been to this shopping centre before, but only ever to Wilkos and Iceland downstairs, never to the mezzanine level where the so-called café is.

Mezzanine makes it sound fancy. It's not. It's pretty run-down, and the café is a token gesture, looking more like a charity shop with mismatched furniture and random boxes stacked around the edges, that just so happens to sell instant coffee and be a hub for the overflow of social services' activities.

The whole thing had been a really stressful experience. I might not have all the post-pregnancy and breastfeeding hormones to deal with at the moment, but my cortisol levels have skyrocketed. Even the logistics of trying to time everything for William's schedule, so he would sleep during the 30 minute journey in the car, without arriving too early – "It's important that you don't arrive too early for contacts," Jo had told us, "so they can stagger your arrival with Stacey and Craig" – and having to make sure he was ready for a feed when we arrived – "don't feed him before contact, so the birth mum can have a go at feeding him," Jo had told us. And then I'd had to hand him over to a stranger in a lanyard and listen to his cries reverberating around the cavernous glass building.

The stranger-in-a-lanyard (a supervisor I'd never met but was meant to trust with my baby) had encouraged me to go do my shopping or take some time to myself, but there was no way I was going to be any further from William than was absolutely necessary. So I'd waited on the shopping centre balcony, staring at the tired, gaudy Christmas decorations hanging from the ceiling.

This turned out to be a good decision, as after ten minutes of incessant crying the stranger-in-a-lanyard – now looking very frazzled – had reappeared and asked me to come and show Stacey how to calm him. I'd felt unprepared to see Stacey again; stress and anxiety instantly claiming me as I'd followed the stranger-in-a-lanyard towards the crying. But my stress had been overshadowed by Stacey who was visibly riled by William's cries. She'd handed him over, avoiding my eye contact, "he won't *fucking* calm down." It had felt strange, yet empowering to be the one to show her what to do. So, I guess I'd left that contact with one gain – confidence that I really do know William's needs.

Needless to say, contacts are not my choice activity, and yet they dominate my week. I have very little control over my time these days. Even if I wanted to go to more of these village hall playgroup things I don't really have the time, with contact sessions and frequent visits from Jo and the health visitor and meetings with William's guardian, solicitor and social worker... It's a hectic schedule.

I have a glimmer of hope that contact may be cancelled tomorrow, given Stacey's absence on Friday for reasons unknown. It was infuriating at the time, having gone through the trouble of getting there only to discover she hadn't turned up, despite saying she would. But it also felt liberating to turn around and drive away again without the emotional strain of having to hand William over.

I'm lost in my own thoughts and don't notice that William has finished his bottle. He cries out, suddenly and loudly, making me jump (despite that fact that his cries are a perpetual soundtrack to my life at the moment and shouldn't come as a surprise).

Everyone's looking at me – the bottle-feeding mum without a birth story – at least I think they are, and I decide it's time to leave. It's not that the mums here are unkind, it's just that life must be very full for them (I get it), and they clearly don't have the energy to make the effort with someone new, especially someone who isn't forthcoming with gory birth details.

Much to my disappointment, it appears that Stacey has remembered to turn up to contact today. I pull up in front of the children's centre – we're meeting in an actual children's centre today – and she's stood outside smoking.

For a moment I consider driving round the block – I'm pretty sure this is what Jo would have me do – but I've had very little interaction with Stacey recently, and despite wishing she wasn't such an intricate part of our life I still want to get to know her a bit and find out whatever I can about her background... about William's background.

At this point we're aware that William is her fourth child, with Sienna as William's only full biological sibling. We gather that all her children are in care, and that she has been homeless at times and has had seasons addicted to Class A drugs, with frequent convictions for stealing to fund her addictions. The details remain quite nebulous for now.

I park up, unload William and his paraphernalia from the car and walk over to Stacey. She lowers her cigarette and greets William, giving him a little pat. She doesn't look at me. For a small woman she has a presence; not a confident, commanding presence, but an aura that smothers those around her with whatever vibe she's got going on. Usually she's irritable and skittish, but today she seems bizarrely collected. It unnerves me.

"'Ow you doin' my little Graydon?" Her voice is slow and slurred. She comes really close to him and I'm worried the smell of smoke is going to agitate him as it has done previously, so I draw him back slightly hoping it's not too obvious.

"Proper good name, innit," she adds. "Named 'im after the policeman who came round when I took an overdose to kickstart labour." She says this so casually. An overdose to start labour?! My gosh.

"Nice bobby 'e was," she adds, now shouting to be heard over the siren of a passing police car – a regular occurrence in this neighbourhood.

She's still not looking at me. What do I say? I opt for, "Oh. Right!" The same as my stranger-friend who was caught off guard by my birth story at the village hall yesterday.

"But you were going to call him William?" I ask, wanting to confirm what she told us on the first day we met. She nods, turning her head away from us and slowly exhaling smoke over her shoulder. I give William a little bounce as he lets out a few shrill cries, disturbed by the siren or the smoke, or both.

Jo's been pretty disapproving about us calling him Willam; we try to refer to him as Graydon when anyone from social services is around, but easily slip up. Changing a child's name is frowned upon in normal adoption but is a complete no-no in Fostering for Adoption because there's always a chance they could return to their birth parents. I understand this, but I think I'm living in a parallel universe to Jo, where William is ours forever. Currently, I can't compute a reality in which he's taken away from us. I hope I never have to. We've known William from two weeks old and I believe we'll know him forever; we want him to have a name with meaning.

We also had an unnerving situation in B&Q in Taunton the other week when I called William, Graydon – having just been on the phone to Jo and being in Graydon-mode – and the man behind us in the queue said, "My nephew just had a baby called Graydon too. Been taken away by social services though hasn't he. Fucking social services." Graydon is an unusual name, and we definitely don't want to risk being recognised by birth family. Everything Stacey is saying right now is simply confirming our instincts and I'm feeling increasingly vindicated in our decision.

But my sense of satisfaction is momentary. She looks me in the eyes, "Bytheway, we're gettin' a place at a parent and child unit. Stopped takin' drugs, 'avn't I. Been clean for weeks now." She looks back at William, "I ain't losin' you Graydon. We're gonna make this work."

My heart is pounding. "Oh. Right!" I say, again. We've been so confident. Now I'm wondering if my confidence is founded on anything. Have we just been believing what we want to believe? Are there things social services haven't been telling us? It can take a while for information to filter down.

I'm about to ask more – desperately trying to regain composure and formulate my questions – when yet another stranger in a lanyard walks out. He looks disapprovingly at us – we shouldn't be talking unsupervised – and Stacey immediately stubs out her cigarette and heads inside.

"You must be Clare and little Graydon?" His voice goes all high and squeaky when he says 'little Graydon', looking at William. I confirm that we are indeed Clare and little Graydon. He takes William in his arms and follows Stacey inside.

I'm left standing there, bewildered.

I want to pick up the phone and call Jeremy, but he left for America this morning on a work trip (poorly timed, but not his fault). I don't think I've ever felt quite so isolated.

One of the questions on our PAR was about our support network.

We had assured Jo that it was strong and well established. Jeremy's parents are nearby, as are Rachel and David; Carol and James moved down last year and are less than half an hour away now; we've got a lovely little church community in the local village (granted they're not in the same phase of life, most of them retired, but all very supportive) and other family and friends scattered around the country. Everyone's been so lovely – our old church in Watford arranged for a load of frozen meals to be sent our way after William came home with us, Pat and Bill have been attentive and loving, Dad and Shirley have come to visit, and Carol and Rachel have popped by when they can amidst the busyness of children and work. But despite this network, I feel so alone. Jo's right, I need a village.

I've always had myself down as an over-sharer, with a tendency to wear my heart on my sleeve; someone who easily connects with people and builds genuine friendships with ease. But at the moment I don't really know what to say to people. When I'm asked how things are going I tend to say something vague like, "Oh, it's a bit hard at times but generally everything's really good!" This statement is true, it's both hard and good. But there is a complex myriad of emotions under the surface that I can't express, including an underlying anxiety that we might lose him. No one around me seems to know how this feels.

I've buried this anxiety with a facade of confidence, but it's just been unearthed by Stacey's comments about going to a parent and child unit. If she has been getting clean drug tests and is getting herself together then there's every chance she's telling the truth. Maybe I should call Jo and ask what's going on.

It's starting to rain so I head back to the car, parked in view of the children's centre just in case I'm needed. I call Jo, but it goes straight to answerphone so I decide to ping her an email instead, explaining what Stacey's told me about the parent and child unit, asking if we've missed something and whether we should be worried.

I am worried.

I've been craving more time to myself, but now I have some time on my hands I don't know what to do, other than sit here and stew. I was planning to do a bit of work in the car while I waited – responding to emails on my phone and getting a bit more on top of my to-do list, but I can't concentrate. Jeremy and I both reduced our hours at work once William was home with us, but it's still a lot to juggle and I'm not entitled to any adoption leave until we get official confirmation that William will be placed for adoption – something called a placement order which first needs to be agreed by a board (the Agency Decision Maker) and then officially approved in court. My colleagues have been amazing – I've even taken him into the office in Clevedon once or twice and he's been passed around and doted on. But I'm still struggling to keep my head above water and find time to get the essentials done, in and around caring for William, contact sessions and all our various appointments with the powers that be.

With Jeremy away it would be handy if I could leave William with Pat for a few hours so I could work or do some basics like washing or hoovering. I know she'd be over in a heartbeat. But not being legally ours I'm not allowed to leave him with anyone. It feels lonely at times and I realise how much I want Mum around – her easy company, her consistency, her gentle advice. I often end up working late at night – sleep seems to be way down the priority list at the moment. Maybe I should sleep now.

I see someone approaching the car. Instinctively I hit the central locking. I don't mean to be suspicious, but this isn't the nicest of areas.

Is he...? He *is*... He is actually undoing his flies... I turn my face away in horror while fully aware that he is exposing himself at my window.

I have no idea what to do, but before I get a chance to think properly I see a policeman approaching from across the road, gesturing and shouting at the man. The man, who the policeman is calling Dave – clearly this isn't their first interaction – makes no attempt to run, but casually pulls up his trousers and greets the officer.

I sit there, frozen. This is not my day.

Once the policeman has cautioned Dave, or whatever he's doing, he comes and apologises to me and takes a token statement. He pauses before heading back to his car, "Just want to check you're definitely ok Mrs. Wilson?" His large, dark, furry-caterpillar-esque eyebrows bunched in concern as he poses the question.

I've been saying 'I'm fine. *Fine*. *really* fine. It's *fine*!' on repeat. Perhaps too much. He seems unconvinced. But has to take me at my word and encourages me to talk to someone should I need to before heading away, muttering something into his radio.

Am I fine? I don't know why I'm saying this. I'm rattled. Ratted by Dave and his wildly inappropriate behaviour. Rattled by Stacey. Rattled by uncertainty. Rattled by an intensity of love for William that overwhelms me and threatens to ruin me should I lose him. Rattled by loneliness. Rattled by an unanticipated, stifling wave of grief for mum, that came out of nowhere and caught me unaware.

I take a deep breath and hold it, fixing my eyes on the door of the children's centre, willing William to reappear.

CHAPTER 10 – Cock-ups

Clare

It turns out Stacey is a prolific liar. She frequently makes offhand comments that instil panic in me. The majority turn out to be unfounded, but always send me into a blather before I've verified the truth. She wasn't about to whisk William away to a parent and child unit. Nor was she teetotal, drinking copious amounts of cider (apparently to contribute to her five-a-day). Nor was she getting clean drug tests, all recent tests showing that she was still using heroin.

I'm baffled and exhausted most of the time, feeling compelled to trust her but constantly dodging her lies. Often the things she says could theoretically be true – she could, theoretically, apply for a place at a parent and child unit at any point – so it's hard to filter her claims, especially when the thought of what she's saying fills me with anxiety and panic. It's almost impossible to be emotionally measured and maintain perspective.

Maybe she can't help it. Lying. An uncontrollable tic. I imagine her being exposed to a culture of lying growing up, a repeated pattern that seeped into her subconscious and become a natural, obvious way of dealing with conflict and life's complexities. I summon some compassion, but mainly feel annoyed by the unfortunate combination of her compulsion to lie and my instinct to trust people and take everyone at face value. I don't think she's trying to trap me, but she's spun a web and I'm gullible prey.

I've barely seen Craig. He's turned up for a few contact sessions but seems to have been in and out of prison recently, charged with assault the last I read. When he's not in prison Stacey seems to drop off the radar, often texting to say she's coming in for contact and then promptly rolling over and going back to sleep. I imagine they perpetuate each other's drug habits when they're together.

The benefit of this lack of commitment on her part is that our contact sessions have been reduced to two a week. It still feels like two too many. If William was going to return to Stacey and Craig then I get how important it is for us to help maintain this connection. But as far as I'm concerned he's not going back, so it feels like an unnecessary stress having my emotions tampered with every Tuesday and Friday. My anxiety fuelled, my frustration stoked. I desperately need the adoption process to move along so I don't have to keep calling into question William's permanence in our life. It's an excruciating emotional rollercoaster. The majority of the time I want to hide from it all, pretend it's all over and that I'm not at risk of losing my child.

All we need now is a placement order for William, to confirm that he will be placed for adoption rather than returning to Stacey's care. Once this order is in place we can stop contact sessions and move forward with the adoption process. It will also mean I can finally go on adoption leave and stop the ridiculous juggling of work and parenting that currently defines my life.

In theory it sounds straightforward, but I'm learning that nothing proceeds without drama, the latest cock-up being that social services missed the fact that Stacey and Craig never registered William's birth. This small, fundamental detail has led to a significant delay in proceedings, leaving us in an elongated state of limbo.

It all seemed to be going so smoothly. In April we found out that the powers that be had finally agreed that adoption is the best way forward for William – cue huge sigh of relief, a tub of ice cream for me and large glass of celebratory wine for Jeremy – which then meant that a court date could be set to obtain the all-important placement order. This was set for 2nd June. I wrote it in capitals on our wall calendar, circled three times, and I was assured that once this placement order was agreed then the rest of the process would be fairly plain sailing. We would go before another official panel called a 'matching panel' where we would be matched as adopters for William (surely a matter of going through the motions rather than anything else!). Following this, there would be another court hearing to approve the adoption in the eyes of the law. The formalities would then be wrapped up with a celebration hearing, an opportunity for us to celebrate his adoption in court, with family and friends present.

I had daydreamed about having William's celebration hearing in the summer, or maybe even late spring, with a BBQ or garden party. Friends and family milling about in the sunshine with wine and snacks; William playing in the grass with his cousins. Forever ours. There's no way all this could drag on past August at the absolute latest. Surely.

So when June came round and we eagerly awaited the lowdown on how the court hearing had gone, and whether a placement order had been issued, we were stunned by the news that the judge could not rule in favour of adoption because William had no birth certificate. Everything delayed because a vital piece of paper had been overlooked. How had no one checked this?! It's not as if Stacey is reliable. Why would she have prioritised registering his birth without a prompt?

I was gutted. An emotional wreck. Jeremy was fuming. In the absence of anything else to do – or anyone to punch – I wrote a strongly-worded email to Jade, toned it down a bit, and then back up again, trying to find a line between angry rant and helpful instruction, if there is one. I appreciate that social services have a heavy workload, and I always aim to be gracious and understanding, feeling phenomenally grateful for all they do, but in that moment we needed the knock-on effects of this administrative oversight to be felt.

I began to doubt how effective my strongly-worded email would be, and whether it was in fact a bit too nice and they might not gauge how pissed off we are. But to our relief Jo stepped in, following up on the issues and echoing our frustrations. When I first met Jo I'd wished she were warmer – not that she's cold, just very professional and appropriate – perhaps I prefer unprofessional and inappropriate? Or maybe it just took a while for me to figure out where I stood with her. It's strange to lay your life bare before someone but get little to nothing back. And she never has 'got' my sense of humour. I joked with her the other day that I should make myself a *What Would Jo Do?* bracelet, "to help me stick to the rules a bit better," after I'd had my wrist metaphorically slapped for offering Stacey a lift after a contact session. I say I joked *with* her, I actually joked *at* her, as she didn't seem to know what to do with my comment and simply reiterated that I should not be offering lifts, or even talking to Stacey unsupervised at all.

But despite not finding the same things funny, as time goes on I'm beginning to realise we got the best social worker out there. She could not be more consistent, reliable or helpful; there's definitely something to be said for being professional and appropriate, so it turns out. Though no amount of diligence on Jo's part can make the social services administrative cogs turn any faster. We knew it would be a while before everything was rescheduled, and a while it's been!

Eight months in fact since we first brought William home. It's now mid-August – when I thought we would be celebrating William's adoption – and yet we're *still* waiting for a placement order. Today or tomorrow we should hear that it has been approved by the court.

I'm constantly refreshing my emails to see if we've heard anything as we drive over to the gardens in Hestercombe, where we're meeting Sienna and her mum, Kate – she's now officially adopted – for the first time. Jo has encouraged us to connect, so William can spend time with his biological sister. I didn't need much encouragement, I'm intrigued to meet them both, and keen to foster a positive relationship for William that builds a bridge to his biological family.

As usual, Jeremy's driving – apparently my driving is sub-standard, something about me not changing gears when I should. I keep having to twist round in my seat to pass things to William who's getting a bit angsty. The combination of this and continually looking at my phone is making me feel a bit sick. This sensation of light-headedness and sickness reminds me of being pregnant. I've not been pregnant since the final round of IVF – for years pregnancy and miscarriage were continuous, but then... *nothing*, just regular periods and a dose of 'normality'. I still think about being pregnant though – more often than I'd like – wondering if it will ever happen again, wondering if my body might change with time and be able to carry and birth a baby. The wondering feels uncontrollable; an addiction that's semi under control but still habitual. Why does my brain do this? A dose of guilt gets thrown into the mix. What is this obsession with pregnancy and birth when I have my own child *right here*? It's too much to make sense of. Maybe I never will.

We're nearly there. I swig some water and gather myself. I hope our rendezvous lives up to expectations. We arrive at the gardens and spot them before they spot us, my eyes are drawn to Sienna's flaming red hair. She's sat in her buggy, legs sprawled, with her middle two fingers stuck in her mouth. She must be somewhere between one and a half and two. A lady with a pink flowery top and dark hair is crouched down, trying to wrestle a red scooter into the net storage under the buggy. Sienna looks straight at me as we walk over.

"Hello!" Jeremy says as we get closer. "You must be Kate."

Kate emerges from behind the buggy, flicking her hair out her face and straightening up. A noise of delight escapes from her mouth when she spots us.

"It's *so* good to meet you!" she says, giving both of us a hug. I warm to her instantly. She seems genuinely excited to meet William, getting down to his level and making him smile; she's what they call 'a natural'. I try something similar with Sienna but she looks away, scowling.

"She's just having a moment," Kate says, "an unauthorised car nap on the way here and she's not come round yet!" She pauses for a second. "Gosh, I hardly know where to start! There is so much I want to ask you both. It feels so good to meet people in the same situation."

She's right, it does. I didn't realise how much I needed this, a chance to chat candidly about all the challenges of the adoption process with someone who gets it (and *really* gets it – she tells us she used to be a social worker, so she's seen it from all sides). She also appears to have degree-level knowledge regarding Stacey and Craig's family history.

Before beginning the adoption process she'd fostered Sienna for a while, so Stacey and Craig visited her at home on a number of occasions. She seems pleased to have had this opportunity to see them up close and personal, and is clearly keen to discover every detail about them by digging back through archives and scouring the internet to build as full a picture as possible.

"Did you know that Craig's grandparents were involved in a murder case?" she asks matter-of-factly over her shoulder as she chases Sienna along the path, now out the buggy and careering around.

No we didn't.

"They owned a social club somewhere in Norfolk, I can't remember the name of the town right now but I've got it written down if you're interested. They found the bodies in the big bins out the back."

I look at Sienna, wondering if she's listening to this and has any comprehension of what her mum is saying. I assume not, as Kate hasn't censored anything so far – giving all the details of Stacey and Craig's crimes and drug use. While we talk openly around William at the moment, I imagine when he's older we'll be pretty careful about what we share when he's within earshot. We want him to know about his birth family, but at an age when he's better able to process the facts.

The family insights keep coming, including that Craig's uncle is a known paedophile. I'm hooked, but also surprised to find myself wondering how much of this I need to know. I'm feeling a rare wave of confidence in the Fostering for Adoption process. What Kate has been through sounds like it comes with a load of complexities. So despite all my frustrations with the process, I'm feeling grateful right now that we've always fostered William with the intention to adopt. We've been Mummy and Daddy from day dot. And although I've sought to get to know Stacey and Craig, this has generally been fairly non-invasive. They may have got under my skin and stirred up unwanted emotions, but I'm glad they've never set foot in our home.

We wander around the gardens for the rest of the afternoon, musing over William and Sienna's similar mannerisms, delighting in their interactions, and thoroughly enjoying each other's company. Eventually we say our goodbyes, each needing to get back in time for kids' dinner; William loses it if he doesn't get his dinner between five and five-thirty. What did I use to do at this time of day? It's only been about eight months since I became a mum but I can barely remember. My life is run by such a tight schedule these days.

On the way home we discuss our time with Sienna and Kate. By discuss, I mean I externally process to Jeremy, re-going over everything Kate has said. As I bring up the grandparent murder case again my phone beeps. It's on *very* loud.

"An email from Jo," I say, opening it and reading aloud to Jeremy.

"Dear Clare & Jeremy, at last we have ratification! I left a message on your landline a moment ago but thought I would e-mail as well in case you don't pick up the phone message quickly. We have a placement order!" I exhale and reach over and squeeze Jeremy's leg.

"I am still awaiting a copy of the placement order from Jade's team before I can submit the Adoption Application but I am chasing it daily. I will need to inform the foster carer placements team that G's placement has become an adoptive one so your foster carer payments will cease. I know that you already know that but just thought I'd remind you. I guess Clare's adoption leave can at long last begin. Your employers have been very understanding and patient. Stay sane and strong. Very best wishes. Jo."

There's much jubilation in the car. And all the complex emotions I felt earlier – the compulsive wonderings about pregnancy and birth – evaporate into nothingness. I'm too busy looking at William and feeling every joyous emotion. *This* little boy, with his quizzical brow – wondering why his parents are behaving strangely, wooping, cheering and grinning from ear to ear – is *my* son. I did not birth him, but he has been grafted into me; he is *of me*. We're one step closer.

I got the Christmas decorations out the other week; unearthed them from the depths of my office-cum-storeroom. If Jeremy could have his way, he'd get the decorations out on Christmas Eve, but I'm a Christmas-decorations-out-on-the-first-of-December kind of gal. So we've compromised with the second week of December, just before my birthday. Our house is now adorned in tinsel, including my naked statue collection in the garden.

Attacking the Christmas tree is currently William's main goal in life. He's obsessed. Eyes off him for a moment and he's *there*; grabbing, tugging, swiping, and squealing in triumph, clearly aiming to bring the entire thing down on his head. We've removed all decorations from the lower branches, but he's not deterred. I'm watching him now, currently occupied with the Duplo. Or so it seems. Maybe he's a genius child and is pretending to play while plotting his next move.

A weight has lifted since we got the placement order back in August. I've revelled in the time I've suddenly clawed back, with no work or contact sessions contending for my attention. It's glorious. I can finally hang out with William without distraction. And now I'm actually getting a decent amount of sleep at night – consequently feeling more human – I have energy for him and experience so much pleasure in getting down to his level and making him laugh.

I've been taking him along to an all-singing, all-dancing baby Makaton class which we both love. He toddles around, clapping, laughing and making the Makaton sign for more biscuits, and I get to chat to my *friend* – finally I have a mum-friend! – Mel. We click; mutually enjoying each other's company. She's a single mum; a total superwoman. I'm in awe of how well she not only copes, but thrives.

Jeremy and I have marvelled at William's development; watching him hit all his milestones with such joy and satisfaction. There is still a significant question mark over how the drug abuse he was exposed to in the womb will manifest itself as he grows, but increasingly we're feeling confident that he'll be ok. I wonder how much the consistency of Fostering for Adoption has helped to settle and regulate him; it must be considerable. We celebrated his first birthday last month with joy and gusto, bulldozing past our feelings of sadness and frustration that he is still not officially adopted. The helium balloon was a particular hit. He knocked it around like a punch bag.

Soon after the placement order was issued we had our matching panel where we were officially matched as William's adopters. We were confident it would be straightforward, especially as we had to take William with us – fostering rules preventing us from leaving him with anyone else – and the panel had never seen prospective adaptors with the child they were planning to adopt before. I'm sure observing us interacting with William, and he with us, worked in our favour, but the panel still didn't make us feel entirely at ease, maintaining poker faces and asking probing questions. In particular they honed in on why we called him William, not Graydon; we really had to fight our corner. I considered what Jo would do throughout it all and muted my sarcasm for the entirety of the proceedings.

But since then, it feels the adoption process has ground to a halt. Four agonising months of *nothing*. It feels like the important decisions have been made: William placed for adoption – *check* – us confirmed as William's adopters – *check*. But *still* we're waiting for all this to be formalised by the court. We gather there's been a hold up with the paperwork that needs to be submitted before the court hearing can go ahead. Jade left last month and William has a new social worker – we've nicknamed her 'the useless one', which is possibly a tad harsh, we are comparing her to Jo's exceptional standards after all – but useless or not, she seems incapable of efficient admin. I can tell that Jeremy has been itching to walk into County Hall and sort out the paperwork himself, baffled by the lack of efficiency. It feels like every other person I see is asking me whether the adoption has been finalised yet – even the cashier in Sainsbury's – and I try not to roll my eyes when I have to explain that there is an issue with *paperwork*... Yes, the same paperwork that has been going on the past three months.

But today things are finally happening. Today is the long-awaited hearing. By the end of today William should officially be adopted. What could possibly go wrong?!

We're not allowed to attend this one. It will be just the judge, Stacey and Craig, their social worker and solicitor, and William's solicitor, guardian and new social worker there on his behalf. So we're waiting at home for news that William has been officially adopted. Duplo building hasn't lasted long and we're now back to Christmas tree grabbing, so I decide to give William an early lunch and get him down for his nap. The hearing was at ten am. It's now eleven forty-five and we've not heard anything. I don't know how to keep us entertained today. The waiting feels slow.

Lunch is messy and short lived. I hope nap time will be more successful. He snuggles in as I carry him up the stairs – a good sign – and I snuggle back, breathing him in. He is so embedded now. Part of us. I can't fathom life before him or without him. I keep thinking back to this time last year. Going to the hospital the day before my birthday and seeing him for the first time. By far and away the most transformative moment of my life. Sacred. It was all happening so fast at that point, we never prepared ourselves for how painfully slow it could become.

While William naps I try to distract myself by searching for elf costumes online – I have a vision for a Christmas card which involves both William and Jeremy in elf outfits. Jeremy hasn't agreed to this yet. Maybe I should pop up to his office and show him the elf costume options. I look at the clock. It's twelve-thirty now, he'll probably pop down for lunch in a minute anyway. *Twelve-thirty.* How have we still not heard anything about the hearing? Surely it should all be done and dusted by now. I ping an email to William's social worker – The Useless One – asking for news.

Over lunch with Jeremy I hypothesise about what might be going on. It was probably delayed by something, or maybe The Useless One's phone's broken. Jeremy nods along, offering no further suggestions, just saying that we're bound to hear something soon. I know he's as on edge as I am, just maintaining composure and sensibility. I tell him about the elf costume idea just before he heads back to his office. He categorically refuses. I'm not deterred. There's time to bring him round.

The Useless One lives up to her name and we don't hear anything back. At two-thirty I decide to ring Jo. Unexpectedly she picks up, and I say a surprised "hello!", despite being the one who called her, grab the baby monitor (hoping William doesn't wake from his unusually long nap – I'll pay for that one later) and dash across the drive to the home office, putting her on speakerphone as I go.

I catch my breath and mouth 'it's Jo' at Jeremy. He gives me a 'why are you being weird?' look and says calmly, "Hello Jo. Have you heard anything from the court hearing?"

There's a pause.

"I'm really sorry..." she begins.

No. I'm holding my breath. Why's she *sorry*? What's there to be *sorry* about? I'm clammy and tense, every muscle bracing against these three words. What could possibly have gone wrong?

"I'm afraid William's social worker and solicitor forgot to turn up," she continues, slowly.

"What?" I bite my lip. I rarely swear, even in my head, but *what the fuck*?! I put my fingertips to my temples wanting to shout or scream like a distressed child. I look at Jeremy in disbelief, but he can't bring himself to meet my eyes.

"Was Stacey there?" he asks.

"She was. And she was looking pretty together today," Jo pauses, aware this information can't possibly go down well, but wanting to give us the straight facts nonetheless. "She's had a series of clean drug tests, so overall she came across quite well to the judge. She's put in a grievance," she pauses again... "The Judge has agreed to challenge the placement order."

I'm speechless. Could we lose him at the final hurdle? I can't bare it; I'm hot with anger and distress.

"I'm so sorry. This shouldn't have happened," Jo says. No it *shouldn't*. "And I'm going to follow up on it myself." She tries to reassure us. We know she's got our backs, but this is an almighty cock-up.

Jeremy says he needs some air, walking out of the office as soon as we hang up, heading for the field beyond the garden.

As if on cue the baby monitor beeps, and I run to William. Down the drive, through the kitchen, up the stairs, two at a time, and scoop him out of his cot. I am *never* letting him go.

CHAPTER 11 – Hope is here

Jeremy

We're biding time in the bus. William is in the driver's seat, relishing the opportunity to tuck his legs under the enormous steering wheel, twisting to the left occasionally to vigorously jiggle the gear stick with two hands. He looks back at me, his passenger, with a look of wild exhilaration and triumph on his face, his untamed Boris Johnson-esque blond hair escaping from under his fur-lined hood, as he releases a noise that's somewhere between a roar and a squeal. He looks like a tiny madman.

I'm trying to be relaxed about the game – whatever the game might be – but this is a 1950 Leyland Olympic bus, my pride and joy, second only to William and Clare of course (Clare would debate this) and it's not a toy. I'm using my 'calm voice', but I'm feeling increasingly stressed, saying a gentle but firm "stop William!" to practically everything he's doing. I repeat the calming mantra to myself, "it doesn't matter, it's an old bus needing restoration," over and over again in my head. It helps. He's only one and a bit, what damage can he actually do? I think, just as he manages to dislodge the indicator lever.

A cold January wind is blowing through the open doors of the barn, straight through the back window of the bus and onto the nape of my neck – the window glass is currently missing, one of many jobs to do in the long-anticipated restoration. I start plotting how to extract

William from the bus and get him back in the house. Why is Clare taking so long?

She's busy gatecrashing the long-awaited adoption court hearing, or rather loitering around outside County Hall hoping to catch word of the proceedings. We've had to wait six weeks for the rescheduled appointment, in which time we've endured mounting uncertainty as five-months-clean Stacey has appealed the placement order in favour of going to a parent and baby unit with William. We gather this request is being seriously considered, seeing as she appears to be making an effort to turn her life around.

Jo has assured us that William's social worker, solicitor and guardian will all be present in court this morning. I asked if I could also attend, for assurance and greater representation. I knew it would be a 'no' but needed to ask anyway – it's hard to be a bystander in something that has such fundamental significance to our lives.

I imagine it's this pressing desire to be involved – or at least close to the action – that prompted Clare to fabricate an urgent need to go to a very specific kitchen showroom that happens to be located two-hundred yards from County Hall at exactly ten-thirty this morning. I know she's hoping to conveniently bump into William's social worker on her way out of court. It can take a while for the outcome of the hearing to filter down to us, and we're tired of waiting, even for an extra few hours, so she's taking matters into her own hands.

I'm hoping Clare will be back with news soon. I spotted her phone languishing on the kitchen worktop, so I have no way of contacting her to find out if her mission has been successful. In the meantime, William and I are sufficiently distracted. Adoption hearing day has coincided with bus delivery day. Until now this majestic vintage bus has been sat in the barn I've been renting in Hampshire with Bob for the last ten years, but we decided it was time to stop neglecting it and give it a new home in the barn in our garden. A low loader lorry bedecked with bus arrived this morning, an exciting spectacle for all the neighbours.

I attempt to lure William away from the gear stick by offering him raisins. He bats my hand with a loud guffaw and the raisins fly in the air and land all over the floor of the bus. He then flings his head back letting out an unrestrained cry of despair. I take a deep breath.

Glancing in the rearview mirror I spot Clare's ginger hair. She's running, possibly skipping into the barn. I stand on the bottom step of the bus, holding a reeling William and trying to read the look on her face.

"So?" I ask with urgency, as she reaches us, leaning on the side of the bus to catch her breath.

"Yes!" she gasps. I wait for her to elaborate. She doesn't.

"The adoption's been granted?"

She nods, a wild, triumphant look on her face, similar to William's moments ago. I want to punch the air, but refrain. "I'm not sure what swayed it," she explains, "but apparently the judge wasn't willing to approve the parent and baby unit, so ruled in favour of adoption." I look at William with his face now red and furrowed, still angry about his raisins and oblivious to the life-altering decision that has just been made. I lift him in the air to make him laugh and Clare cups his face and kisses him as he comes back down.

"You're *ours!*" she declares, "actually *ours!*"

It feels surreal, yet utterly natural at the same time. How could he be anything other than ours? Our relief and joy is palpable; this is the most elated I've ever felt. I continue to jiggle William up and down, his furrowed brow now replaced with an exuberant look, I imagine similar to mine.

"Don't worry, I was very stealthy and didn't bump into Stacey or anyone," Clare says, climbing past us onto the bus, skirting round the engine protruding from the floor and gathering the scattered raisins, as if on tidying-up autopilot mode.

I nod, adding, "I'm sure you were." I'd never describe Clare as 'stealthy' but there's a first for everything, so I give her the benefit of the doubt.

"I just chatted with Tina, y'know, William's new social worker," she adds. It's hard to keep up with all the new names. Thankfully The Useless One didn't last long. "She didn't tell me much, other than the fact that it all went pretty smoothly in the end. Though she did mention that the judge ruled in favour of letterbox contact – y'know, exchanging letters with Stacey – but I'm sure that will be ok."

"I'm sure it will," I say, nodding, appreciating the potential value of this for William in the future, but also feeling a nervous at the prosect of future contact – even if just through the letterbox. Stacey sent William a Christmas card this year that was very pointed, saying something like, "To *my son* Graydon, Happy Christmas, I love you so much *my* son – etcetera – love *your* mummy.' Clare in particular found it uncomfortable, dutifully keeping it, but stashing it away out of sight.

"Anyway," Clare interrupts my thoughts, not wanting to derail us from the joy of the moment, "Tina said we should have the paperwork through in a few days. I can't believe this is actually happening!"

Clare joins me and William in a family hug and we jump up and down nearly toppling over, while Clare whoops with delight. We want to celebrate. But now we've arrived at the moment we've been waiting for we don't really know what to do with ourselves. We discuss options – cake featuring in all of them.

As we wander back to the house Clare says what I've been thinking.

"I'm *so* relieved... but I kept thinking of Stacey as I drove home. I feel sad for her."

I wouldn't have put it quite like that; I don't think I'm sad, per se. But as we discuss what sort of cake we'd like to celebrate with, I'm imagining Stacey standing outside County Hall, cigarette expertly balanced like an extension of her fingers, contemplating the reality of having lost yet another child. Our victory is her defeat. It's an uncomfortable reality.

In the weeks following William's official adoption we begin preparing for his celebration hearing; an opportunity to meet the judge who's been involved in the case and get friends and family together to celebrate. I can tell that the thought of Stacey is niggling Clare like a dull, uncomfortable pain in the lead up to the event. I know it will pass, but also wonder if it will always stay with us in some way; loss and gain coexisting... one impossible without the other.

It seems that everyone we know wants to be at the celebration hearing; a converging of lives that's not happened since our wedding. And when the day arrives the courtroom is full. We stand in front of everyone, in our Sunday best under the royal coat of arms, with the judge announcing the formalities of William's adoption and officially handing over his certificate. William is nestled snuggly in my arms, swinging his legs and enjoying the attention. The ceremony is succinct, extended briefly by our friends John and Penny, from my childhood church in Petersfield, offering to pray for us and a few others bursting into spontaneous song; it feels appropriate and poignant. The judge has clearly never witnessed anything like it; I forget that there tends to be a touch of the bizarre when charismatic Christians get together.

We all decamp to a gastropub round the corner, where we've hired a room and organised a buffet. Ross and Beth – Carol's kids – sit on the floor with William, showing him how to push cars along the wooden floorboards, while the rest of us mill about sipping wine, eating tapas and exchanging pleasantries. There's a little cluster from social services gathered in the corner. They were surprised when we invited them, which in turn surprised us – they've been so integral to navigating us through turbulent times this past year, it would feel "odd to celebrate without them," as Clare had put it.

The occasion marks the start of a new era; where things in many ways continue as normal, but without social services looking over our shoulders or the dark cloud of uncertainty above our heads. It brings a sense of liberation, but is equally draining, as if our bodies have been in a subdued state of perpetual crisis for the last year. It takes a surprising amount of intentional energy to decompress. There's also a substantial shift in mentality required; it feels unnatural not to seek guidance from social services for every decision or meticulously document and report every bruise William gets.

As the months begin to pass without the frequent drama and calamity we've become accustomed to, we start to ease into our rhythm as a family of three without fear that something is going to happen to disrupt the balance. We feel gratitude – bone-deep gratitude for a life we thought we'd never live. It's stronger than any other emotion, and permeates the days that also feel exasperating, tedious and exhausting, allowing us to deeply enjoy life, the mundane days as much as the exciting ones.

We search for shells on the beach and etch his name in sand; drive around on my lawnmower, even when the lawn is perfectly mown; hold a dedication service for him, as a communal way of acknowledging our gratitude to God for his presence in our lives;

share our bread with the ducks, letting them eat out our hands; gather with my family for Sunday roasts and totter around with Grandma Pat in her garden; navigate tantrums and off-days and energetic bouncing-off-the-wall days; celebrate William's second birthday with balloons and cake and wine for me, and a few months after we celebrate his adoption day – his 'Gotcha day' – with family, and reminisce with so much joy. We revel in the present.

"I can't believe how much mess he makes!" Clare exclaims one evening, laughing yet exasperated by the carnage and perpetual need to tidy up. It's late January and exceptionally cold. We've spent most of the day inside and the state of the house shows it. "Imagine how much longer this would take if we had more kids!" She's throwing Brio train tracks into a box in the living room, projecting her voice so I can hear her from the kitchen. I had been listening to the news headlines on Radio 4 while making a curry, but the description of Turkish police discovering a stolen Picasso painting is drowned out by Clare's very loud external processing.

"I just cannot *fathom* how Rachel and David do it! *Four* kids! I mean... It's a lot isn't it... And I know we always talked about having four, but imagine the chaos. It would be *chaos*! And I would be here tidying up Brio tracks 'til midnight every night! Seriously. Even with *one* more it would be mental!... Imagine *double* the mess!"

She hurls some more tracks across the room into the box. Why can't she just move the box closer?

"Wilson? Hello, are you listening?"

"Yes, intently to every word!" I shout back. "I just didn't think you were asking a question."

"Well... I guess not. But anyway. It would be *mad* wouldn't it." It's still not really a question but I 'mmm' loudly in agreement. She throws some more tracks. "But also nice too..." she adds after a brief pause. "And I guess it probably wouldn't be *double* the mess would it. Just a little bit more. And I'm tidying up anyway, so I guess I could tidy up for two. Or more, maybe..."

She trails off. There have been times in the last year when we've talked about going through the adoption process again. Naturally thinking about the future; our minds subconsciously exploring the territory ahead. They've tended to be brief conversations. Despite a mutual understanding that we'd love to have more children, the thought of adopting for a second time has made us both shudder; the inevitable intensity, uncertainty and long, agonising process. Every time it's cropped up we've parked it, not quite ready to make a decision, while also practically held back by being told that we can't adopt again until William turns two.

But as time has gone on, providing distance and space to recover, our conversations on the topic of adopting again have become more optimistic – this one on the trials of tidying aside. I sense we're re-acquiring enough mental stamina to go through it all a second time.

Clare appears in the kitchen doorway. "Do you think we should sign up again?" She says, in her quiet, I'm-being-serious tone. "I mean, at least just to get the ball rolling, y'know. William is two now so we can technically do it and I guess, y'know, I wonder what we're waiting for."

"A little tidying elf to move in?" I suggest.

She rolls her eyes. "No *really.* Shall we?"

"What's a bit more mess?" I say, smiling at her over my shoulder before adding some cumin to the curry.

The next morning Clare signs us up. If feels a bit mad to have made such a significant decision so casually. Of course, the build up to this conversation has been nothing but casual – months of pondering, healing and careful self-assessment of our emotional and physical capacities. But the moment that clinched it was ordinary; just a regular Tuesday evening, tidying up Brio and agreeing that mess is annoying but totally worth it.

Much to our relief we are immediately assigned back into Jo's capable and reassuring care. We're keen to go down the Fostering for Adoption route again, which Jo seems positive about. Some updates are made to our PAR document and Jo works through some scenario's with us as a reminder of the 'dos' and 'don'ts' of fostering, in particular revisiting who has parental responsibility while fostering. We're quizzed on who can agree to immunisations during this time – *the birth parent* – and who decides on what baby milk to feed the baby – *the birth parent* – and whether it's permissible for a friend or relative to babysit – *no.* It's a sobering reminder of the autonomy we denounce when going down the Fostering for Adoption route. Clare attends a few refresher workshops where she takes incoherent notes to pass on to me – we've somehow persuaded Jo that this is thorough enough to tick the necessary boxes.

As anticipated, it feels like a breeze this time round, but despite the simplicity of the process, it takes six months before we are invited to attend a panel meeting and are formally approved for Fostering for Adoption again. So by the time we get the stamp of approval in July we're ready – really ready. Clare has sorted out some of the baby equipment; setting up the cot and making sure the bottle steriliser is in good working order. "Remember what happened last time," she said, a playful note of warning in her voice, "we went to the panel and then three days later we were holding William."

She's right. That's exactly what happened, and we were woefully unprepared. But it makes the waiting this time round, with the empty cot in the corner of our room and drawers full of baby clothes, feel jarring and somewhat agonising. There is no excited whisper of a newborn baby from Jo in the days after our panel, and months later we're still waiting.

By October we decide to sign up to Link Maker; an extensive database of children awaiting adoption, with profiles from across the country. William is nearly three now, so we could look at adopting a child around the age of one – maintaining the required two year age gap – through the traditional adoption process, rather than going down the Fostering for Adoption route. Fostering for Adoption is still our preference – we loved nurturing William from newborn – but we're losing hope in another Fostering for Adoption opportunity coming available, so we're widening our options. It feels strange and unnatural when Clare and I discuss such profoundly important matters in such practical, logistics-focused ways, and stranger still when we start looking through this database of children; scrolling through in the same way we would when online shopping, but with a whole lot of emotion involved.

"What are we doing?" Clare asks one Saturday morning in early December, absentmindedly putting more and more pancakes on William's plate while scrolling through Link Maker on the iPad with her free hand. "How are we meant to just *pick*? And also, *why* is it proving so impossible to adopt when there are so many children here needing a home?! Argh."

I don't think she actually wants an answer right now, and William is filling any silence in the room with a constant cry of, "mooooore pancakes, Mummy! More more mooooore!" So I continue making coffee and add some general noises of engagement and interest.

It's not that I don't echo the questions she has, just that I have no answers. We're both starting to feel weary of it all. How is waiting so exhausting? The Christmas decorations are soon to come out *again* and it feels we've got nowhere this past year.

Clare turns the iPad off and pushes it away, turning her attention to William just in time to grab the maple syrup off him before he douses his pancakes.

We expressed interest in a little girl called Sadie a few weeks ago. As is Clare's way, she became very attached to the little we knew of her. It seemed that things were progressing as they should until yesterday, when Jo called to say that the process was cancelled as they wanted to find a match for Sadie in Manchester, where she's from. Clare was devastated and is still reeling from it now.

"Maybe we need to stop." She's bustling around the kitchen now. I leave the coffee brewing and stand next to her at the sink, putting my arm around her shoulders to physically slow her down.

"What do you mean?"

"Just not adopt again," she says quietly, almost in a whisper. She's looking over to the corner where the bottle steriliser was – we put it away a few months ago, it felt like it was tempting fate. Not that we believe in fate. "Maybe we just need to be content as we are, us three," she adds, "rather than living waiting and wondering what tomorrow will bring. I'm tired of it."

"Let's see how we feel in the new year, shall we?"

She nods silently, heading back over to William who's starting to climb on the table in an attempt to secure the maple syrup.

"Leave him with me," I add, retrieving William who arches his back in frustration shouting "no Daddy!" and then starts climbing onto the table again as soon as I put him down, giggling cheekily with a 'catch me if you can' glint in his eye. I see it's now a game. "Oookay," I say slowly, wondering how to diffuse this one without a tantrum ensuing.

"Why don't you get the Christmas decorations out today?" I say to Clare, while plotting my next move in the maple syrup 'game'.

"Early?" She's surprised. As am I. These words have escaped from my mouth before I've realised. Perhaps they're betraying the fact that I've found myself thinking about a spectacularly gaudy Christmas display outside a house I passed the other day, complete with an inflatable Santa and light-up reindeers on the roof. Christmas decorations have always been Clare's domain, but I've been wondering whether to get involved and crank it up a notch. Fairy lights on the front of the house? A giant inflatable snowman in the front garden?

Clare doesn't wait for my reply before adding, "Ooooow and we could do our annual elf picture today too!" This seems to be becoming a tradition now; one Clare takes great delight in at my expense. Her equilibrium has been restored – possibly swinging too far in the opposite direction – as she skips off towards the barn in her dressing gown to locate the elf costumes, while I absentmindedly watch William drizzle copious amounts of maple syrup on his pancakes and plot how to introduce a giant inflatable snowman into our life.

We said we'd take stock in the new year. It's now early February. If it were down to me, I think I'd just continue waiting; something is bound to happen soon. But Clare is tired; ready to stop waiting and start living.

It has felt like a particularly painful sort of waiting. At one point in time we waited monthly, wondering if Clare would get pregnant or not. But for the last six months, since we were approved to adopt again, we've waited daily – will we get the call to say a baby has been born? Or a reply saying we're a potential match with a child we've spotted on Link Maker? – every day bringing with it a small dose of disappointment that has accumulated into a mountain that we tend to scale and descend every twenty four hours. It's tiring and tedious and completely out of our control. I like to think God has a plan; I believe in a God who cares about the vast and minute matters of this world, and chooses to interact with us. But, yet again, I sense his absence – I don't know what he wants for us going forward, and I don't know what I think anymore. My faith has morphed into something very stripped back and child-like. I wonder if this is actually what faith is meant to look like – raw and real – but it's unnerving.

I can tell Clare is feeling defeated – too much waiting, too many prayers that feel like they've been lost in the ether. She's not herself at the moment – tired, more irritable and making fewer jokes, a clear sign something is wrong.

"I've lost hope," she says one night, as we lie in bed, looking over at the cot she set up in July last year. I don't know what to say, but agree that enough is enough; if hope is lost, then we need to put an end to this limbo. We decide to ring Jo in the morning and tell her we're happy as a family of three.

But come the morning I can tell Clare is procrastinating. She's washed the breakfast dishes, put a clothes wash on, dusted the ornamental fairy houses above the Aga, and is now playing an urgent game of 'rappers' with William, who was previously playing happily on his own. There is nothing standing in the way of her calling Jo.

"Shall I do it?" I ask.

"Do what?" She says, pausing from her rap about cheesy puffs.

She knows what. It's hard to take her seriously when she's dressed like a rapper. "Call Jo and tell her we're pulling out."

"No, I'll do it. I'll just finish this game first."

I raise an eyebrow, unconvinced.

Conveniently, her phone rings and she starts rummaging through her coat pockets trying to locate it. More opportune distraction, so I leave her to it and head out the door and back to my office, coffee in hand.

I've barely got started with today's overwhelming email inbox, when Clare appears at the door looking mildly hysterical, hotly pursued by William whose wellies are on the wrong feet.

"What is it?"

"Jo!" Clare heaves. So she's called her.

"What was her reaction?" I ask, thoroughly confused by Clare's demeanour. I was anticipating a crestfallen Clare today – at peace with our choice but dejected as she comes to terms with it, making up raps with William about how unfair life can be. But here she is, a frenzied look on her face. Has she actually gone mad?

"No!" Clare says, looking at me as if I've asked a ridiculous question, as William climbs on my lap and starts hitting the keys on my laptop, asking whether he can have a sip of my coffee. A caffeinated three-year-old?! "No!" I say to him, with more force than I anticipated. He grabs the mug anyway, which I then have to wrestle from his hands, coffee sloshing all over my trousers.

"She called *me!*" Clare continues, seemingly oblivious to the scene unfolding before her. "A baby was born four days ago. Jo thinks she's the perfect match for us."

She stops to take a breath. I look at her in disbelief, letting William have full control of the mug.

"Jeremy, her name is *Hope*."

Less than twenty-four hours later we're standing at the reception desk of the NICU in Yeovil District Hospital. There is a lot of activity going on around us – I can't tell whether some crisis is occurring or if they're just seriously understaffed. The receptionist said, "with you in a few minutes," about ten minutes ago. She's intently staring at her screen, frowning and huffing and puffing, occasionally popping a heart-shaped chocolate in her mouth as fuel for the task.

Clare moves to the left to accommodate a couple of nurses who are trying to access the chocolate box from across the counter on their way past, and in doing so somehow gets tangled in the string of a heart-shaped helium balloon. This has the benefit of getting the receptionist's attention, who had apparently forgotten we were there.

"Oh yes," she says. "You're here for..."

"Hope..." I say, suddenly realising we know nothing else about her, no surname or any other details. "We're Jeremy and Clare Wilson, her foster parents?" My voice rises at the end like it's a question, when it's not. I'm looking over my shoulder half-expecting Jo to appear as she often does at critical moments, despite being aware that she's not meeting us until this afternoon. I'm caught off guard by my own words. Are we her foster parents? Is this actually happening? I'm half expecting someone to tell us that a mistake has been made.

"Ah, yes. You can wait over there." She nods towards a few plastic chairs the other side of the general bedlam of staff and visitors.

We sit down and I'm about to whisper, "Happy Valentine's day, by the way," to Clare – who is attractively blowing her nose profusely into an inadequate pre-used tissue she's retrieved from her pocket – and apologise that the card I bought her hasn't yet found its way out of the drawer in my office and into her hand, when the receptionist shouts over, "Oh actually, you can go straight in. Down the corridor, to the left. Ward B."

The ward is spacious and bright, with low dividing walls providing some separation between the babies lying in plastic boxes masquerading as cots. We've barely finished explaining who we are to the slightly frazzled looking nurse on duty when she exhales "great," and points us in the direction of the cot directly opposite her desk, asking if we can change Hope's nappy and give her a bottle, muttering something about being very busy and understaffed today.

Hope is tiny. She's dressed in a pink Winnie the Pooh baby grow and, unlike William, she's free from wires and tubes and seems to be sleeping peacefully, despite the pooey nappy we're catching whiffs of. We change her nappy as instructed, just before another nurse arrives to inform us that we're just in time for Hope's bottle and if we follow her she'll take us to a private room where we can have "a bit of space".

"I'll carry her," she adds, putting a hand out to stop Clare from picking Hope up, as if she's not capable of carrying a baby. "You can have cuddles once you're in the private room."

On the way, she explains that Hope is displaying some signs of neonatal abstinence syndrome – although, from what we can see, the symptoms seem to be very mild compared to William's – and needs close supervision, but is otherwise doing really well. We're encouraged.

"You've come on a good day," she adds as she ushers us into the room. "It changes the atmosphere when the police are hanging about." She then hands us a bottle and leaves before we have a chance to ask why on earth Hope has police protection.

We exchange glances, but turn our attention back to Hope, taking it in turns to give her the bottle and take some pictures of her to send to Carol, who's waiting expectantly at home with William. We're undisturbed for an hour and a half – a blissful hour and a half of attuning ourselves to Hope; soaking her in and adjusting our minds to this surreal turn of events – until the same nurse returns, abruptly explaining that they plan to discharge Hope today or tomorrow.

"You need to leave now," she instructs. "Hope's birth parents are on their way. We'll let you know when she's discharged. Someone from social services will deliver her." We discern that it's not the moment to quiz her further on the police presence, so we kiss Hope and take our leave.

Back at home – via another trip to Mothercare – we hurriedly prepare ourselves for Hope's arrival. While I'm unearthing the steriliser again, I get a call from the hospital to say that she *will* be discharged today and someone from social services is coming to collect her 'soon'.

We debate what 'soon' means, agreeing that in social services terms this probably means anytime in the next couple of hours, "or months!" Clare jokes. It's now one pm, so factoring in the hour's drive from the hospital to our house, we conclude that she will probably arrive between three and four.

Clare keeps thinking of more things we need to find – the baby bath, various bouncers, baby toys and blankets. This continues for a few hours, with Jo appearing in the midst of the chaos saying she's been reliably informed that Hope has been picked up and is on her way to us *now* – we calculate her ETA as three forty-five latest. With fresh motivation for the final push, we continue with the baby-preparations, me drawing the line at getting out the jumperoo – this will clearly not be needed for another six months – and then declare ourselves ready.

The doorbell rings at three pm making us all jump, despite knowing that Carol is about to drop William home. He saunters in asking where his sister is.

Jo frowns at us. We've been told to be careful in how we describe who Hope is to William. We are "just fostering" her at this stage and should not be referring to ourselves as Mummy or Daddy, or to William as a sibling. Clearly we've crossed this line already by explaining to William this morning that we were going to the hospital to meet his sister (although we never said anything about bringing her home today – that's his own assumption).

Jo clearly disapproves, and I appreciate why, but it felt like the best way to explain what's happening to a three-year-old. We will embrace Hope as our child; William needs to know that she's part of our family.

Three forty-five comes and goes and we all begin to wonder what's going on. By four-thirty Jo is making various calls, eventually discovering that Hope has been taken via County Hall so that her chaperone can pick up some paperwork.

Clare is up in arms about this – we all are – "She's *five days old*!" She reminds us, "sat in a car seat for hours... we could have gone and picked her up if we'd known!"

William is getting angsty, picking up on the unusually pregnant atmosphere and annoyed by the fact that he was hoping to have dinner with his new sister at five o'clock.

By five fifteen he's eating chicken nuggets on his own, enjoying Jo's company, having seemingly forgotten about his date with Hope (three-year-olds are fickle) when the doorbell rings. Clare is stood within arm's reach of the front door (where she's been stationed for the last two hours) and opens it before the 'dong' of 'ding dong'.

"Are you Clare Wilson? I've got a baby for you," says the man on the doorstep, scooping Hope out of the car seat and handing her to Clare before she's answered.

"And here's their stuff," he adds, putting a small bin bag of belongings just inside the door.

"Really sorry, but I've got to dash. I'm on holiday now and off up to Manchester tonight to see my girlfriend. Valentine's day n'all that. You just need to sign... here." He points to a dotted line on some paperwork he's just handed me. I sign and he goes without a backward glance, as if he's just delivered an Amazon package... not a baby.

Clare brings Hope inside. Silently we gather around. William wriggles in between my arms, climbing on a chair to get a better look, and Jo stands at a distance, present but not intruding on our moment.

The door is still ajar, cold air infiltrating the warmth of the kitchen, but we don't notice. We just watch her, even William is silent, instinctively appreciating the weight of the moment.

I wrap my arms around him as I look at her, so still and peaceful. "Welcome home, Hope," I whisper.

CHAPTER 12 – Tenterhooks

Clare

We find ourselves in familiar - yet totally new - territory. This time, rather than truncating the traditional nine months of baby-prep time into just four days, we've had to shoehorn it into less than nine hours. It's been three days since she arrived on our doorstep and we've descended into chaos.

I'm stood in the doorway to the kitchen with Hope in the sling over my Christmas pyjamas – which I have now been in for 24hrs and *must* be changed into actual clothes today rather than fresh pyjamas – surveying unwashed crockery strewn all over the worktops and William's toys cascading in from the lounge. He seems to have managed to get out everything he owns – which is an alarming amount – how does a three-year-old have so much stuff?! I can't see the laundry from here, but I know it's spewing over the side of the basket, which is where it will stay – festering and growing in size for the foreseeable future. I make a mental note to add my Christmas pyjamas to this pile once I'm out of them, and put them away somewhere once clean. It is February after all. Christmas is well and truly over.

William was sat happily at the kitchen table a few moments ago, pushing a couple of trains around while he waited for his toast, resembling a civilised human being. But he is now dramatically wailing on the floor because Jeremy cut his toast into triangles, not squares. Small children are a curious species. I watch with morbid fascination for a moment, unable to snap into action and wondering whether I can go back upstairs and pretend I never came down.

"Please confirm I'm not going mad." Jeremy's spotted me. He certainly looks like he's going mad. He's usually fairly calm and collected but the last three nights have consisted of a series of short naps rather than anything resembling a good night's sleep. He's a shadow of his usual self this morning. "It's *triangles* that he likes, isn't it? Not squares. It's always been *triangles*."

"Well it's clearly not," I say, unhelpfully. Adding, "Your mum cut his toast into squares yesterday and he's decided that's what he likes now."

"Well thanks for passing on that important piece of information." He puts a fresh slice of bread into the toaster and attempts to tame William.

Perversely, after having been up all night, Hope is now peacefully asleep on my front. I'm worrying that William's raucous cries of, "I want SQUARES," might wake her, needing to retrain myself that virtually nothing can stir a newborn when in the depths of sleep. If you can get them to sleep that is, which we seem incapable of achieving at nighttime.

Her drug withdrawal is not as acute as William's, but she's still suffering; crying for long periods, shaking at times, startling herself when she drifts off and then tensing and reeling from the discomfort.

The last three nights we've taken it in turns to hold her, pacing up and down the landing, swaying with the rhythm of her cries, telling her she's safe, we love her and she'll be ok. It's hard to know what she needs – I'm floundering. Is this lack of intuition normal? I imagine with a child you've carried and birthed you have this sixth sense of what they need. Surely. Although Rachel assures me this isn't true; "Everyone feels like they're drowning at first," she told me when I was out of my depth in the early days with William.

I repeated her words to myself last night as I kept offering Hope a bottle, willing her to latch on and stop crying – *everyone feels like they're drowning*. I know it will help when we get into a rhythm with feeds, giving us a sense of what she needs, but at the moment her cries all sound the same – a plea for *something*. I'm giving her everything, but it doesn't feel like enough.

I glance at the clock. Seven forty-five. Somehow we need to be out the house in an hour to drop William at pre-school and then get over to County Hall to meet Hope's birth parents. William's still mid-tantrum – the triangle toast seemingly ending his world – we're all still in our pyjamas and no one has had their breakfast. I need to do some sort of Houdini action and get dressed with Hope still asleep in the sling – there's no way I'm waking her. I wish I could just rock up at County Hall in my pyjamas without raising any eyebrows, or calling into question my suitability as a foster carer and prospective adopter.

And now I'm starting to panic about feeds and whether I should wake Hope and feed her now. Or do I wait so she arrives at Country Hall hungry and wants to take a bottle from her birth parents, as I've been instructed to do. But the thought of a sad Hope in the car is torturous. I pause in the doorway of the kitchen for a tad longer, paralysed by how overwhelming the daily task of getting dressed and out the door feels. I turn around and go back upstairs. I could at least attempt changing my bottom half while Hope's asleep in the sling. A step in the right direction.

It's a miracle that we're in the car and heading out the drive at eight fifty-six; largely down to a dream combination of Jeremy snapping into action, getting bags packed and making all the decisions that I can't – like, we should wait to feed Hope at County Hall and transfer her from the sling to the car, *still asleep* – and Fireman Sam on telly to placate William. As expected, the risky transfer did not work and Hope is crying, which has prompted William to put his hands over his ears and shout 'lalalalalala' at the top of his voice to drown her out. I'm not sure if I've brushed my teeth, they feel furry. I'm pretty sure I did, but then again, that could have been yesterday morning, it's all blurring into one.

It's less than a ten-minute drive to pre-school, but it feels like an age with the lala screaming shenanigans in the back. Thankfully William loves pre-school and I feel a wave of appreciation for his wonderful teachers who scoop him up on arrival, ready to give him a dose of structure and normality for the day. I linger for a moment watching him go in, wondering how this mad weekend has felt from his perspective. His world's just been invaded; his parents commandeered by another tiny human. He didn't ask for this, or prepare for it. He has very little comprehension of what's going on. This is partly why we've decided to opt for simplicity in referring to Hope as his sister. He can't compute the complexities of the process; that she's part of the family, but may not be forever. I feel choked.

Back at the car, Jeremy's bent in an awkward position stroking an apoplectic Hope. He straightens up as I get in, driving off before I've fully shut my door. I think we both still have mild PTSD after enduring William in the car as a baby – he hated his car seat and would scream like he was being tortured. But thankfully the motion calms her and by the time we reach County Hall she's asleep again.

We sit for a moment, soaking in the silence and bracing ourselves for the unknowns of the next few hours. I'm anxious about meeting Hope's birth parents. Interacting with Stacey was a significant emotional and mental drain; her presence a constant reminder of the uncertainties and unknowns we lived with. And even now that William is adopted and we don't have to see her, I still feel wary. A sense of unease. She will always be in our life, even if just as a name in William's story. In *our* story.

At the end of the adoption process William's social worker presented us with a Life Story Book, which tells the story of his birth family and why he was adopted. It's meant to be presented in a form that a child can grasp, but I'm not sure how any child could begin to comprehend the complexities of drug addiction, or the concept that you can be loved but not safe, or that you can be placed for adoption and still be so wanted, or that you can belong so wholly in arms you weren't born into. Stacey and Craig's faces stare at us from the second page – like mugshots in a lineup (I wish William's social worker had tracked down better ones). One day we'll look through this with William. I'll want to physically hold his emotions. Cradle them. Protect him from feeling anything other than loved beyond measure. And wanted. So wanted.

"We should probably head in," Jeremy sighs, neither one of us possessing the energy to shake hands with two more individuals who are about to become an intricate part of our story; the people who could one day lead to us losing Hope. Jeremy gets the buggy out of the boot while I carefully scoop Hope out of her car seat. She stirs, but I draw her close, pinning her to my chest to still her startled body. Miraculously, she stays asleep. I breathe her in. The last few days have been overwhelming, but I would not change it. And I'd live in this chaos forever if it meant keeping her. Jeremy draws next to us, picking her hat off the floor and gently putting it back on her head. Kissing her softly.

I didn't have time to contemplate the eruption of love I'd feel for this child; this child who we didn't even know existed this time last week. It's caught me off guard. Floored me. The thought of losing her already feels inconceivable. I marvel at how regular foster carers manage the emotional turmoil. Perhaps some master the art of governing their emotions; able to lovingly engage without investing their whole self. But my whole self is all in, despite the situation being precarious. I can't find a middle way – we must love her as ours from the start and face the unbearable consequences should we lose her.

We're directed to a room in County Hall. My heart quickens. I'm getting flashbacks to the first time we met Stacey and Craig. This encounter had better be less off the wall. At least we *know* we're meeting the birth parents this time – that's a good start.

I spot her as soon as we walk in the room. She's short. Dark, greasy hair pulled back into a high ponytail (or perhaps it's hairspray – not grease – it's got that crusty hairspray effect). She's wearing a hoodie, jeans and Converse trainers. I catch her eye. She has a slight bruise on her cheek – healing but still visible. She smiles at me. Her eyes narrow as her smile widens, but not in a suspicious way. She seems soft. Inviting.

Hope's social worker introduces herself, Hope's guardian, and the contact supervisor. All three names go in one ear and out the other. "And this is Tegan, Hope's birth mum, and Nate her birth dad," she continues. I repeat their names again in my head in an attempt to retain them. "And Clare and Jeremy, her foster carers," she gestures towards us. I wave awkwardly, while Jeremy confidently steps forward to shake their hands. I notice Tegan is glancing towards the buggy. Hope is stirring.

"And Hope, of course," I say, adding Hope to the introductions, despite her being the reason we're all here and needing no introduction. She's our one thing in common. Our gatherer.

Tegan approaches the buggy, glancing at me as she does so, seemingly seeking my approval. "She'll be hungry if you'd like to feed her?" I invite. She crouches down, her face close to Hope. Nate draws in too – he seems tough; hench and covered in tattoos, but he catches my eye and smiles as he strokes Hope's cheek. I'm disarmed. There is so much tenderness in this moment; I'm in this scene, right next to them, holding the handle of the buggy tightly with my left hand, and yet I'm an onlooker. I get this strange sense that I shouldn't be part of this. It's unsettling.

The next forty-five minutes pass calmly. I don't know what I was expecting, but it wasn't this. I chat with Tegan as she feeds Hope, hearing about the birth and filling her in on our last few days. I find her endearing. She's intuitive with Hope; responding to her cries and quietening her with ease. But she also seeks my advice, asking me how I hold her when winding and if I persevere with the bottle when she seems to dribble everything out. It softens me.

The only awkward moment is when she complains about her boobs hurting – too full of milk – and asks if she can feed Hope to help relieve the discomfort. Hope's social worker – who I now gather is called Lindsay… I think, or Linda – swoops in. "No you can't feed her. Your drug tests have been positive," she says bluntly. "And she's not your child." It feels like a really harsh thing to add. Lindsay or Linda is also pregnant, which I know she can't help, but it feels a tad insensitive to have assigned a pregnant woman as a social worker in a case where another woman has just lost her baby. I smile awkwardly, hoping to reassure Tegan, who nods acceptingly but is visibly disgruntled.

We sit quietly together for a moment and I overhear Nate talking to Jeremy about their older children. Two boys, both in care. I'm baffled. This couple seem so… normal. Inoffensive. What on earth have they done to have had three children removed from their care?

"I always wanted a girl," Tegan says, gazing at Hope and stroking her head. I open my mouth to say something, but my words are lost somewhere between my brain and the air. So I close it again. Sitting silently. My heart aching for her. I wish it wouldn't. My emotional reserve is so depleted at the moment, but I seem to have no control over how it's spent. It leaks uncontrollably, and I find myself unintentionally invested.

Nate comes over to us, closely trailed by the contact supervisor, and asks if he can hold Hope for a bit. I notice some tension – at least I think I do – as Tegan passes her over. She clearly avoids his eye contact, tightening her lips, and moving away, biting her fingernails and looking out the window. Maybe she doesn't want Nate to hold her? But he is equally as lovely with Hope – rocking her and smiling at her. I find myself looking away, unable to cope with the intensity of the moment; the proximity of love and loss.

Amidst my compassion for Stacey I'd also felt contempt; a lack of respect that verged on disgust at times. But I'm not feeling that now. My feelings towards Tegan and Nate are unexpectedly and overwhelmingly positive. Which just makes this whole situation excruciating. I cannot root for them. Their gain would be my loss. I must guard against feeling too much for them.

I'm sat in the car outside the children's centre where we come for contact, waiting for Hope. The sky is dark and heavy, the wind whipping the leaves and blossom on the ground into a frenzy; not very spring-like. I glance at my watch. Hope should have just finished her hour session with Nate, switching to her hour with Tegan. They have separate sessions, feeding my suspicion that they're not together anymore.

It's a long morning for Hope, repeated three times a week. The frequency feels intense. With the half hour drive either side, it takes a good three to four hours out of our day and messes with Hope's routine, which we've finally got her settled in. I spend the rest of the day figuring out where she's at and what she needs. At least it's always at the same children's centre; a significant redeeming factor! I don't have to hold the extra information about where I'm meant to be going each day in my head, as I had to with William. I have no surplus brain capacity these days.

From where I'm parked I can see past the brick walls surrounding the centre to the covered area outside reception. As expected, I see Nate emerge for his post-contact cigarette. He braces against the unseasonably cold wind, hunching his shoulders and lifting his hood. I feel a fondness for him; he's approachable and genuinely engaged with Hope. He seems to love his time with her, making it about her rather than fulfilling a need he has. At least this seems to be the case. I respect him for that. Tegan too. Their ease with Hope makes it easier to hand her over, knowing she'll be tenderly cared for.

Hope's significantly less distressed than William was at three months old. William would be visibly agitated after a contact session, sensing the unease of the arms he was in, and easily triggered by the bright lights and smell of stagnant smoke. But not Hope. She seems to take it all in her stride – even more so than me. I've been caught off guard by how settled she is, having psyched myself up for another baby who would cry uncontrollably and fling me into a state of near-constant stress that I'd use all my remaining energy to control or suppress. But in reality it only took a week for her to fully come through her withdrawal phase, and now, a few months later, she's thriving and we're revelling in her company; enjoying her frequent smiles and babbling sounds. The whole experience feels novel.

There are still some health concerns regarding Hope's eyes and head circumference though. No amount of good nature can detract from the fact that she was exposed to a dangerous amount of heroin when she grew in Tegan's womb. We noticed her eyes early on. She finds it hard to focus, with one eye noticeably turning in; eyesight issues are a common side effect of neonatal abstinence syndrome, so we've been told. The health visitor has also flagged Hope's rapid head growth, something her social worker – who I've confirmed is called Lindsay not Linda – seems concerned by but hasn't relayed why. She's asked us a lot of questions – weird questions, like how long we leave Hope lying on her back and how quickly we respond to her cries. We're trying not to worry about it. But I can't help but feel uneasy.

We're also sensing our ground is shifting again with William. As soon as we find a groove, we're thrown off kilter and have to adapt again. At the moment I feel that all my instincts are off; unable to pre-empt what William needs, his behaviour unpredictable and all over the place. Is it just that he's struggling to adjust to having a sister? Is it belated terrible twos? Is it more than that? At one point we thought he was out of the woods; a 'normal' toddler, having fully recovered from the abuse he suffered pre-birth. But recently we feel hyper-alert to the potential long-term consequences. His attention shifts constantly. It's hard to engage him in anything for more than thirty seconds, even his beloved Thomas the Tank Engine trains. Is this normal? I have no idea.

When I dropped him at pre-school this morning, his key worker said it would be, "really good if we could have a chat sometime this week", something about needing to understand his behaviours better so they can meet his needs. I'm pleased she's suggested this conversation, whilst also feeling overwhelmed at the prospect of absorbing more complexities in my life, however helpful the outcome might be. How many times a week – a day! – will I feel so monumentally unprepared for parenting? I take a deep breath, slowly exhaling and momentarily closing my eyes. I need rest; deep rest that no full-night sleep can cure. I need to crawl inside a hole and hibernate for a month.

When I open my eyes I notice Nate craning his neck to spot my car. He gives me a cheery wave. I'm breaking lots of rules at the moment, including having sneaky chats with Tegan or Nate when they're outside smoking. I'm not meant to, but Lindsay and the contact supervisor are both inside, none the wiser, and I feel a bit antisocial sat in my car. Plus I enjoy chatting to them and I feel I know them a bit now. I see them more regularly than anyone else at the moment. Jeremy says I'm becoming attached. I was cross with him for this comment; I'm not willing to acknowledge any truth in it.

Nate beckons me over. I hesitate before getting out the car, thinking about Jeremy's attachment comment. I'm not attached... but maybe I'm more invested than I should be. I can't seem to help myself.

It's cold outside. I reach into the back of the car to grab my cardigan.

"I've got somethin' for your little William," he says as I approach, smiling and pulling a Thomas the Tank Engine jigsaw from the plastic bag he's holding. "I got it from a charity shop. But don't worry I've checked, it's still got all the pieces."

"Oh!" I'm caught off guard. What a phenomenally thoughtful gesture!

"It is Thomas the Tank Engine that he likes, yeh?", a look of concern coming over his face.

"Yes! He'll love it Nate, thank you *so* much." I'm so touched I can feel it in my throat, catching and threatening to creep up and form tears. It doesn't take much to make me cry these days. I gather myself. "It's so kind of you."

"Na, no problem. Saw it and thought of your William. No big deal." He stubs out his cigarette despite the fact that he's not finished with it. So considerate.

We continue chatting. He shows me some recent videos of his two boys, sent from their foster carer via his social worker. I wonder if the younger child has additional needs. He's three and a half, but his speech is basic and stilted and he doesn't seem to be walking confidently. Neither Nate nor Tegan have talked about this. Perhaps it's too painful. Nate mentioned last week that the boys are about to be adopted, but that the decision was unfair and 'rigged'. I can't fathom what they must be going through at the moment, and find myself empathising with him, wishing he'd won, whilst also hoping for the same 'unfair' outcome for Hope.

I fill him in on Hope's developments. He's animated. Visibly delighted in hearing about her progress. Nodding along. Cooing when I show him pictures of Hope's first trip to the swimming pool.

"My mum's said she'll help out when we get Hope back," he says unexpectedly, acting as though this is good news for me too. He's told me previously that he's living with his mum again, confirming my theory that he's not with Tegan anymore. "I reckon that I could get custody and manage great with her support. Nearly finished my forklift driving course n'all. Clean drugs tests. Tickin' all the boxes... Model citizen," he adds, winking.

I'm smiling and saying something about how great this is, but feel as though I've been flung into a state of panic. Both Tegan and Nate have alluded to getting Hope back, as Stacey had with William, but this is the most direct comment so far. My growing respect and appreciation for them both has made me feel worried – they clearly love Hope, I can't imagine what would lead the court to rule against them keeping her – but I've supressed these anxieties, giving them as little headspace as possible.

Now Nate is adding something more concrete to my concerns. And this is the first thing he's said about his mum being invested in Hope. This alarms me too. If Tegan and Nate are denied custody, then social services will look for a suitable, willing family member before considering us as adoptive parents. I'm suddenly desperate to have Hope back in my arms. I'm seeing mountains forming ahead of us.

"They must be nearly done," I say, desperately needing a way out of this conversation.

"Thanks again for the jigsaw!" I add over my shoulder as I slip into reception, where I have a few minutes to stew until the contact supervisor emerges with Hope.

The heavens open seconds after we drive off. I have a sudden urge to drive and keep driving. Desperate to escape the future and the inevitable eruption. I can't lose her. I won't lose her. I think of Tegan and Nate, mirroring my feelings. Hope is the rope in a tug of war. I must protect her from this.

Visibility is poor, but through the torrential rain and manic windscreen wipers I spot Nate standing at the bus stop. There's no shelter. He's soaked to the bone. I'm pulling over, not conscious of my decisions, just responding. I roll down the window.

"Can I give you a lift somewhere?" I shout over the sound of rain and traffic.

He runs round to the passenger door and gets in, directing me towards Taunton town centre. He thanks me repeatedly as he gets out, and I drive off wondering how I should tell Jo about my latest faux pas. I'm going to get more than a slap on the wrist for giving Nate a lift. I could just not tell her, but I know I will – some sort of compulsion to tell the truth. I wish I wouldn't sometimes.

As expected, Jo was horrified that I had given Nate a lift. Even more horrified than she was last week when I took Tegan on a shopping trip to big Tesco to get some clothes for Hope. Tegan had been saying how sad she was that she wasn't able to get baby girl clothes, and I'd been planning to spend our foster carer allowance on clothes for Hope anyway, so suggested she came along to choose them. I don't know why I suggested this. I also don't know why I gave Nate a lift. I don't mean to break the rules, I just struggle to find the line between being compassionate and law-abiding.

Jo described Nate as a 'violent man', saying that I had put myself in a vulnerable situation while crossing a line, reiterating that the rules are in place for a reason and I should refrain from any further unsupervised contact. My main takeaway from this conversation was mulling over the description of Nate as a 'violent man'. Violent?

I'm thinking about this as I am standing outside the pre-school gate, waiting to pick up William. He seems so gentle, and it comes across as a bizarre choice of word. Is there something I don't know?

Hope's in the buggy, awake and looking around. A few of the other mums waiting at the gate have gathered round, cooing over Hope and talking about how intense the early months can be and how well she seems to be doing. I'm nodding along, only half listening.

"How's the court case going?" one asks.

"Oh, fine," I say. "Well actually, we're still waiting for a decision to be made. It's all a bit up in the air at the moment." I'm trying to keep my voice light and breezy, but saying this out loud feels agonising.

"I'm guessing you've seen this?" the same mum says, getting her phone out her pocket and showing me an article open on her browser. 'Couple on trial for neglect and abuse' it reads. I take the phone out her hand, without asking, scrolling down and scanning the article. Intrigued, then stunned.

"No names are mentioned," she continues. "But there's reference to a baby girl. Hope would be the right age. Maybe it's about her parents?"

I don't reply. I'm scrolling down in disbelief. Surely not. She's right, no names are mentioned. It's totally incongruous with everything I know of Tegan and Nate – the intentional abuse detailed here is horrifying. But there is reference to two boys in care. The ages are correct. The area they live is correct. And there is a brief reference to a baby girl born a few months ago. I can't process what I'm reading, willing myself to find a fact that rules them out. But so far it's adding up. This is Tegan and Nate.

CHAPTER 13 – An unexpected bump

Clare

I've been sitting at the kitchen table for the last half hour. William's watching Fireman Sam and Hope's sat in her bouncer chewing on Sophie the giraffe. My laptop's open in front of me, but I'm staring past it at the photo-wall beyond – a selfie my dad took of him and William; one of William on his balance bike; another of Jeremy and William dressed up as elves – swimming in and out of focus. I'm desperately trying to find space in my overcrowded brain. It feels like there's a physical fight going on in there, or a surge at an overcrowded punk rock gig. My lungs are compressed. My feet off the ground. Amplified shouting in my head. But I'm sat here in silence.

There are nine tabs open on my laptop. Local news. National news. They're all about the same couple. I cannot compute their crimes. I've just got off the phone to Jo who's confirmed my suspicions. These articles are all about Tegan and Nate. She urged me to be cautious and not to dig too deep online, "You know all you *need* to know," she assured me. I certainly don't *want* to know all I've discovered in the last half hour, but I do feel I *need* to know it. I needed to know it months ago when I first met them. Months ago, when I first became so uncontrollably embroiled in their lives.

I am not to blame in this situation, but I'm turning on myself. I should have been more aloof. I should have refrained from getting so emotionally involved. I should have followed the rules and communicated through social services. Am I really such a phenomenally bad judge of character? What is this I feel? Ashamed? Ashamed for having been so drawn in by their manipulation and lies? Ashamed for being so determined to see the best in them? Should I be more guarded with my empathy?

But they seem so genuine. You can't put that on so consistently. I must have seen *something*. *Something* innately loving and honest that drew me to them, softening my interactions and feelings for them. I think of Tegan, picturing the way she cradled Hope, whispering love in her ear, nuzzling her little face. I think of her wide smile and the times I saw her blink back tears. I think of Nate, so endearing and thoughtful. The Thomas the Tank Engine jigsaw is strewn across the table next to me.

What happened to them to lead to such incomprehensible crimes? How on earth can love and abuse sit adjacent? And what is this empathy doing still creeping into my heart? How can I feel anything other than utterly appalled? Their crimes are so abhorrent. There is no excuse. I'm pulsing with anger and yet still aching with distress *for* them. Why?!

I think of the video Nate showed me earlier today when we stood together outside the children's centre; his little boy with limited speech and mobility because of him and Tegan. Injected with cocaine and then abandoned for hours on end. Subject to physical and sexual abuse. Neglected. Underfed. Twice over for both of their little boys.

Their little faces swim through my mind. And then I think of Hope among them. I physically wretch. I'm back from my trance, slamming my laptop shut, pushing my chair back from the table and gathering Hope in my arms. I take her through to the lounge and sit on the floor next to William, stroking his hair as he snuggles in.

Amidst the confusion and the mess of my mind, one thing is abundantly certain. My whole being is unreservedly devoted to these two little humans. I will face my imperfections to love them as fully, as beautifully, as I possibly can. I will protect them with all I have. Nurture them with all the grace and generosity I can muster.

My unrestrained mind is now thinking of Mum, and how she must have felt about me and Carol. My unfettered heart is aching. My chaotic emotions unleashed. I'm sitting on the floor, clutching my children. Silently sobbing and absentmindedly watching Fireman Sam rescue little Norman Price from the floods in Pontypandy.

Over the next month, Jo feeds me more of 'what I need to know' as Tegan and Nate's trial takes place, and I fill in the gaps by reading online. They plead guilty to having *wilfully assaulted, ill-treated, neglected, abandoned, or exposed two children in a manner likely to cause them unnecessary suffering or injury to health*. The case is temporarily adjourned. According to Jo the judge is keeping all options open, including an immediate prison sentence.

As I reflect on my interactions with Tegan and Nate things start to make sense. I spot signs; things I ignored at the time that seem so obvious now. Police presence at Hope's birth; Tegan's bruises a sign of the domestic abuse taking place; Nate and Tegan having separate contact sessions; the fuss over Hope's head circumference; social services turning up en masse for contact sessions; Jo describing Nate as 'violent'.

Since finding out about the trial, I stay in the car during contact sessions, parking with the entrance to the children's centre out of my eyeline. Minimising interaction with them. I don't know how to be, or what to say. When I do inevitably bump into them, I keep our conversation light and brief. Perhaps they know I know.

But by the end of June a placement order is granted for Hope, which means no more contact sessions and a much-needed dose of stability. I'm at the checkout in Sainsbury's when I find out, Jo calling while I'm desperately trying to multitask; piling all my shopping on the conveyor belt while negotiating with William, who is alternating between pulling Hope's hair and trying to climb out of the trolley. Maybe I should have called her back later, but we always pick up to Jo. So amidst the stress of the supermarket situation, my phone pinned precariously between my shoulder and cheek, I absorb what Jo's saying with relief. A degree of anxiety over losing Hope has lifted, and I'm elated at the thought of not having to go to contact sessions three times a week. I also make a mental note never to go to the supermarket with both of them again. The cashier calls me 'brave'. Brave... or daft?

A goodbye contact has been arranged for Tegan and Nate to see Hope one last time. Stacey didn't turn up to hers, so I don't know what to expect. I've been told by Jo that both Tegan and Nate are coming. I'm relieved Jeremy will be with me for this one. He's less emotionally entangled; able to maintain calm and perspective, whereas I'm a hot mess.

Recently we received an incorrect file from social services – the full version detailing Tegan and Nate's backgrounds, rather than the redacted one. Both grew up in broken families, with parents addicted to drugs and a distinct lack of stability and love. Nate's father was physically abusive, and Tegan describes being neglected and left to fend for herself. I think of them now, sat in the dock, accused of heinous crimes. And then I imagine them both as children and teenagers, floundering in a hostile world, born into a life of drugs and abuse, with no one to lovingly nurture them into a brighter future. My compassion sits alongside my indignation and anger. I try to mix the two together, but they separate out like sour milk in hot coffee.

When we arrive at the children's centre to drop off Hope we're told that Tegan and Nate have invited us to join them for the two hour session. I must seem visibly surprised as the contact supervisor confirms that this is very unusual.

The room we're in is more like someone's sitting room than the meeting rooms we're used to; sofas, beanbags, a coffee table, and shelves piled high with children's books. Tegan and Nate are warm when we arrive. I find it surprisingly easy to hand Hope over; their unguarded demeanours and affectionate interactions with Hope leading me to somehow forget about the ongoing trial and see them as fellow humans.

They chat away to her and to us, finding toys to engage Hope and singing little songs to her. I pull out a pot of pureed apple for Tegan to give Hope. "She's nearly six months," I explain, "I was planning to start weening her soon, so thought you might like to give her a first taste of apple."

Tegan seems moved by this small gesture, and I wonder if she's about to start crying. She lifts Hope up in front of her face, encouraging her to balance on her little chubby legs. All I see are the creases around Tegan's eyes and a furrowed brow – is she crumbling, or smiling? I look away.

Lindsay invites Tegan and Nate to decorate a canvas with their handprints next to Hope's. There's an awkward moment when Jeremy, attempting to assist Hope with her painty hands, knocks some paint over. As is often the case, it isn't Jeremy who makes the moment awkward, despite being the paint spiller, it's me exclaiming 'Wilson!' without thinking, which results in a sharp look from Lindsay at my foolishness in revealing our surname. It's important that Tegan and Nate don't have any information which could lead to them tracking Hope down in the future. I'm mortified, but both of them seem engrossed in making their handprints.

Nate writes, 'daddy', next to his, and Tegan writes 'mummy'. I don't dwell on this, simply enjoying the moment and revelling in how well things seem to be going.

"You can't write that," Lindsay barks, breaking our flow. "Jeremy and Clare are going to be her mummy and daddy." I love being described as Hope's mummy, especially by a social worker *and* before our matching panel has taken place, alluding to Lindsay's confidence that we'll be matched with Hope.

But this comment feels petty and unnecessary. Jeremy clearly feels the same as me as he looks at Nate and Tegan and says, "Oh no, don't worry. We don't mind if you write 'mummy' and 'daddy', you're an important part of Hope's story." But Lindsay proceeds to add the word 'birth' in brackets in front of their names, rubbing salt in a wound. I see Tegan's lip twitch. She gets up and moves away as if to restrain herself.

Towards the end of our time together, Lindsay asks me and Jeremy to leave the room so Nate and Tegan can say goodbye. "Please stay," Nate interrupts, unexpectedly. "We're in this together."

I'm touched, and nod, but I don't want to stay to witness this tearing apart. I'm already crying, desperately trying hard not to. I blink back the tears, attempting to ignore the intense pain in my throat. This is not my grief, it's theirs. But I feel their loss so acutely.

I've been so looking forward to contact sessions finally being over, imagining celebrating after this one – me tucking into a cake, Jeremy cracking open a bottle of red. But there is nothing to celebrate. I cannot celebrate this loss, however much I'm gaining from it.

Nate is saying to Hope that he'll never forget her, and that he's sorry, and they will always fight for her. Tegan is saying how much she loves her. That she'll always love her and will always want her.

I want to pause the world for a moment and focus on *this.* It's beautiful. In isolation, it's beautiful. I want to zoom in so that everything else – the abuse, lies, manipulation and neglect – is out of focus, and this is all I can see. There is love in this moment. Honest love. I want to capture it. Bottle it. Show it to Hope one day. Somehow help her know that it was never about her being unwanted. She was always *so* wanted, by so many people.

Tegan hands Hope back over to me and gives me a hug.

"I've had my first clean drugs test this week," she tells me. "I'm turning my life around. I'm going to get Hope back." Her words aren't aggressive, she just needs me to know. She needs to say it out loud. She needs her final words to be fight.

"I'm proud of you." The words come out my mouth before I've really considered them. Pride is the last thing I've felt the past few months since finding out about their crimes, and the last thing I expected to feel today. But I do. I feel proud. She's lost everything, and yet she's finding the strength to turn her life around.

She's silent for a moment, a tear spilling from her thin eyes.

"No one's ever said that to me before," she says, in a barely audible whisper.

I'm running sand between my hands, Hope sat between my legs, our large floppy sunhats providing a degree of shade. There's less cloud cover than I thought there would be today, but the sun on the sea is beautiful. It makes me think of Mum – she loved the way the sun made the sea sparkle. And after she died everyone spoke about how much she sparkled; her personality so bright and infectious. It was such a lovely way to describe her. I wish she could have heard.

William is careering around in his own little world, waving a spade. I can tell it's a sword not a spade right now. Mum would have been running around with him – joy-filled and unhindered. I make a mental note to come here more often, despite it being overrun by tourists in the summer. The space for William to run and scream unreservedly is liberating. I feel such pleasure watching him in his elation. Back at home it can feel like he's cooped. Like his beautiful, darting mind has to be channelled and controlled. I want to help him find expression for it; to find ways of being his true self, whilst being able to cope with the demands of daily life and society.

We went to the GP with him last month, after a chat with his key worker at pre-school, and he's been referred for an ADHD assessment. We're pleased, ready for help in understanding his needs, and eager to have an EHCP (Education, Health and Care Plan) in place before he starts school next September.

But I found my confidence knocked, wondering how I hadn't spotted this earlier. Berating myself for my lack of intuition. Having wild thoughts about whether I'm the best mother for him.

He races towards us and I brace for a greeting so enthusiastic it could be painful. But he skids to a halt, crawling up to us on his hands and knees like a dog, and licking Hope playfully on the face. It's been hard for him to adjust to Hope being in his life. He's kicked back, loudly and wildly, demanding our attention. But simultaneously he seems to revel in being a big brother, doting on Hope, cuddling her, chatting to her, and getting a huge kick out of making her laugh. He's doing it now. Rolling around in the sand, looking at her. Pulling funny faces and wiggling his bottom. On cue, she laughs. It's the best sound in the world.

Last week we met Hope's biological brothers at the playground just above the beach. It had been another glorious day, the August sun hot on our backs. Jeremy and I had met the boys' adoptive mothers, Jill and Amanda, once before. A lovely couple; clearly emotionally resilient and resourceful. I felt in awe of them.

"We knew what we were taking on," Jill had said, in reference to Hope's brothers, who's needs are multiple and complex. I wondered if knowing their needs in advance made it easier. I imagine nothing could have prepared them. They didn't elaborate.

At one point the eldest asked if he should 'use tongues' when giving Hope a kiss. Thankfully Amanda jumped in so I didn't have to answer, clearly addressing a common problem. "Sorry about that," she'd muttered afterwards. "The poor little love is so confused. His early life was so shocking, he has no idea what's appropriate..." We stood in silence, watching them for a moment. "I wish I could change it for them, but I can't," she'd said. "We're just hoping they can gently heal and relearn as they live life with us in a loving and stable way."

We'd talked about Tegan and Nate's sentencing, or lack thereof. It ended up being very light. A fifteen-month prison sentence, suspended for two years should they not reoffend. This sentence, understandably, outraged Jill and Amanda. Jeremy and I can see how futile it would be to put them behind bars just as they are making significant attempts to turn their lives around – both having had multiple clean drugs tests and finally being in secure jobs. But there is an agonising sense of injustice for the boys.

It felt more acute and painful when I came face to face with the consequences of Tegan and Nate's abusive behaviour, watching Jill and Amanda's beautiful boys, smiling with the sun on their faces, but forever carrying the weight and distress of early abuse at the hands of those who were meant to protect them.

I arrive early to pick up William from pre-school so I can get the best parking spot right outside the gates. This way Hope can stay asleep in the car while I hop out to meet him. That's the plan anyway. He's been back for a week following the end of the summer holidays and so far things seem to be going remarkably well. Perhaps he needs and enjoys the regularity and rhythm of the pre-school day.

I'm enjoying a moment of peace, tempted to close my eyes but knowing that I'll drift off as soon as I do, and wake feeling even more groggy. I need to push through until my head can hit my pillow, which will be moments after the kids are in bed tonight.

I'm knackered. Hope's not sleeping well, so most nights involve one of us – usually Jeremy – sleeping on the floor of her room holding her hand through the bars of her cot.

We had the matching panel last week and are now so close to formally adopting her. We're waiting for final confirmation that we have been approved as adoptive parents, and then we can complete the paperwork and formalise everything with the adoption hearing.

There were times when I never thought we'd make it, and I'm desperate to push this adoption over the line. To change her name to Hope *Wilson*, and be at her celebration hearing hanging out with all our friends and family, rejoicing in her being ours forever.

It's very still right now. No breeze, which is unusual for this hilltop village. The little school and pre-school are at the end of a cul-de-sac. No cars are passing. The other parents are yet to appear.

I'm soaking in the peace and experiencing fresh appreciation for this place. It's quaint and picturesque, and the surrounding landscape is stunning; what school playground looks out over cascading fields and hills as far as the eye can see?

Sometimes it feels a tad too small-villagey here, everyone knows everyone's business – a far cry from the anonymity of London. But there's something to be said for feeling known, I think, as the first parent appears walking up the hill, giving me a cheery wave before disappearing into the school reception.

A commotion outside the house to my left breaks my trance-like state. I can't quite make out what's happening, tall trees and a bush masking the front garden.

The house that protrudes from behind the trees looks ominous, black stains across the dirty white pebbledash, as though the house has been licked with fire.

There's often musings at the school gate about the suspicious goings-on in the house – rumours of a man running an illicit brothel which, of course, no one believes. Just a bit of juicy gossip for this quiet village.

I don't mean to be nosy, but I crane my neck as a group emerge through the rickety white garden gate. Three men and a woman. I freeze.

Rumours or not, this doesn't look good. I feel deeply uncomfortable for the woman who is clearly being manhandled. I stay in the car, wishing I knew how to react quickly and effectively in moments like this. I want to run to her defence but I stay sitting, watching from afar, wondering what to do and whether this warrants alerting the police.

It could be nothing... perhaps I'm overreacting.

I watch the woman, impatient to see a sign that she's ok. She looks really familiar, with her thin figure and feathery ginger hair. There's something about the way she moves, which makes me feel like I know her. And then, as the men manoeuvre the woman to get her into a car, I see her face.

Stacey. It's *Stacey*. I have an overwhelming urge to get out of the car. I *know* this woman who is being mistreated. But if she sees me here she'll know where William goes to school. She'll know we live nearby. I don't move. Then her long cardigan falls open as she gets into the car and I see an unmistakable bump.

She's pregnant.

CHAPTER 14 – Fierce love

Jeremy

Clare practically falls through the door of my office. Hope in her arms and William in tow. I'm in the middle of a video call; thankfully with a colleague rather than a client. It so happens that my camera is perfectly angled to capture my flustered wife and her unruly entourage coming in. William has already scaled the filing cabinets by the door. The few hours after pre-school are a bit of a wild time for him – our theory is that he keeps a lot of feelings pent up and then unleashes them when he gets home. Either that or the teachers whip him into a frenzy just before pick-up.

"Want to call me back in ten?" Marcus asks, helpfully.

"So sorry! So sorry!" Clare is apologising profusely. "We can leave and come back later!"

Can you? I think to myself, as Clare desperately tries to extract William with Hope still tucked under one arm. It looks like leaving isn't an option right now.

"I'll call you back in ten," I agree with Marcus, ending the call. "What's up?" I ask Clare, interrupting her barrage of apologies.

She rapidly fills me in on her sighting of Stacey at the school gates.

"Pregnant?!" I don't know why I'm surprised. But my immediate thought is of the consequences of *this* pregnancy. This unborn baby is William's sibling.

"I rang Jo straight away," Clare says. It's what I would have done too. Jo would know what to do. "She's going to pop round now so we can talk about it – I think she could tell I was a bit shaken up. She said social services are unaware of the pregnancy. Apparently Stacey hasn't registered it yet," she continues, without stopping for breath, "which doesn't surprise me, despite clearly being quite far along in the pregnancy. Jo said they're going to follow up, though I doubt she'll tell me any more at this stage. She seems more concerned about the fact that Stacey has been spotted outside William's school – I'm guessing that's what she wants to talk about."

"This could have consequences for us," I state the obvious, but Clare doesn't reply. It seems clear to me that we will be the first people social services approach if this baby is to go into care, which I imagine it will – us and Kate, Sienna's mum, as we've adopted this baby's siblings or half-siblings. But I can tell Clare can't process this right now; she's emotionally overloaded and at capacity. Perhaps beyond capacity.

I'm looking at her, pink-cheeked, tired-eyed. Her untamed, short, ginger hair giving her an air of eccentricity. I love this look. But there is something heavy in her expression at the moment. The situation with Tegan and Nate has invaded the remaining space in her mind, stealing her emotional reserve, muting her light-heartedness and good humour. Maybe another baby would be too much.

"Are you sure she didn't see you?" I ask, turning to my other concern when faced with a lack of response to my first. "It's not ideal if she's involved with someone who lives *right next to* William's school..."

"No, she definitely didn't see me," Clare confirms. "And I've told Jo, and alerted the school too, so they can be aware." We hear a car pull into the drive, parking in the space just outside my office. "Must be Jo. Thank goodness for Jo." She passes Hope to me, clearly forgetting I have a call in less than ten minutes – I guess Hope will just have to join me – and herds William out the door, who is delighted to spot Jo's car and bounds straight over to her.

In early October everything comes to a head. We get a call from Jo to say that we've been unanimously approved as Hope's adopters. All that needs to happen now is some paperwork and the adoption hearing, which Jo has alluded to being a formality more than anything else, considering Tegan and Nate's convictions.

Meanwhile, the inevitable conversations are taking place as to whether we'll foster (with the view to adopt) Stacey's baby once they're born, although no one knows when the due date is – it could be any time from late November. But in order to take in this baby, we would need to pause Hope's adoption.

Currently, we're registered as foster carers. If we go ahead and adopt Hope now, we would need to reapply to be foster carers in order to take in Stacey's baby, re-attending the necessary courses and working through all the paperwork again, which could take months. During this time the baby would have to stay elsewhere, leading to a distinct lack of continuity for them; something we desperately want to avoid for the child's sake, and a reason why we love the Fostering for Adoption model so much.

So do we pause Hope's adoption and take the baby in as soon as they're discharged from hospital? Or proceed with Hope's adoption and consider adopting this baby at a later date, through traditional adoption methods? Or simply accept that we're at capacity with two children? We're trying to explain the intricacies of all this to my family over Sunday lunch at Rachel and David's.

"Is there no way you can adopt Hope while maintaining your status as foster carers?" Rachel asks. "It seems a bit inflexible.... But then again, I guess if there are systems in place..."

Rachel is the head teacher at a local primary school, so she knows all about needing to maintain systems that are there for good reasons, even if it can lead to a lack of flexibility. She seems to have answered her own question, so I just shrug in reply. Our conversation is being significantly hampered by William, who is under the table pretending to be a dog. Rachel and David's kids, meanwhile, are significantly older and seem to be able to sit at a table and use knives and forks like civilised human beings. I try coaxing William out from under the table, but my efforts are half-hearted. At least the dog antics mean I can have a conversation of sorts with Rachel, even if we're having to project our voices over his barking.

My mum is holding Hope on her knee at the other end of the table. She has a remarkable capacity to embrace and absorb our chaos, despite it being worlds away from the ordered environment she expertly conducted when Rachel and I were young. She used to be a childminder, often having three or four extra pre-schoolers in her care, entertaining them and tending to their needs while also being present and available for Rachel and I throughout our school years. She's a natural, currently doing an impressive job of keeping everything out of Hope's reach – seven months is a prime age for grabbing and swiping and Hope's got her eyes determinedly set on the salt and pepper grinders.

Hope is so attentive to everything since getting her glasses. They were fitted last week following numerous appointments with the Ophthalmologist, establishing that her sight is worse than anticipated. She's been diagnosed with Partially Accommodative Left

Esotropia – in layman's terms, her left eye turns inward – and Bilateral High Hypermetropia – a problem with the eye's ability to focus – and Amblyopia – also known as 'lazy eye', when the brain fails to process inputs from one eye. This is likely a consequence of the pre-natal drug abuse. Hope's glasses are tiny; round and pink, resembling miniature goggles. I wonder what it must have been like for her when she first put them on. She looked straight at Clare and said "mama" for the first time. Her world came into focus. Clare was in pieces. I decided it wasn't the moment to remind her that Hope's been saying "dada" for a month already.

"We would, of course, be a hundred percent behind you if you went ahead with this," Rachel says, in the next quiet moment.

"Yes!" my mum says loudly from her end of the table. I didn't know she was listening. "We will support you in whatever you decide, Jeremy."

My dad roars playfully as William grabs his leg from under the table, and he catches my eye and smiles, confirming his quiet, unwavering support of our wild decisions. William crawls up onto his lap and I watch the two of them, a wave of deep appreciation consuming me. We've told a few of our friends about potentially taking in another baby, sounding them out as we try to constructively think through a very emotional decision. We've been met with mixed responses, a number of our friends voicing that they think we're mad for even considering this. It makes me feel all the more grateful that I can bank on the unwavering support of my family.

Clare begins collecting the plates. Rachel protests, but Clare continues. The same kindness-battle occurs every Sunday.

Clare is unusually quiet today, especially during the latest conversation about pausing Hope's adoption and potentially taking in another baby. She's hesitant, verging on resistant, while I'm feeling very clear about what we should do. Our desires are rarely this out of kilter, and on this occasion our approaches are also out of character. Clare usually makes the more emotionally powered choice, while I ask all the questions about how it's actually going to work in practice. But this scenario has turned the tables. I'm rolling with my emotional hunch – we must pause the adoption and take in William's half-sister – while Clare is wondering how on earth we can pull this off.

She was unnerved the other day, spotting Stacey again outside the pre-school gate. We've tacitly discovered through Jo – who could neither confirm nor deny, but her pointed look said she could confirm – that Stacey's been prostituting herself for drug money, and that the white house opposite William's school is owned by a known paedophile. How a known paedophile has managed to secure a local authority house opposite a school is baffling. Clare's rattled by this – on high alert every drop-off and pick-up.

But she was even more perturbed when she bumped into Stacey in Taunton town centre. There are nearly seventy thousand people living in Taunton, and we rarely frequent it. The odds of brushing shoulders with Stacey are extremely low. But she did, with Hope in the buggy and William walking alongside. We haven't seen Stacey since William's contact sessions ended years ago and she hasn't replied to any of the letters we've sent her – as agreed by the judge in William's adoption hearing. But now, in the space of a few weeks, Clare's seen her *three* times. On this occasion, Stacey spotted Clare immediately, crossing the road to talk to her and peering round to try and catch a glimpse of William – or "Graydon", as she was saying – who had taken refuge under Clare's skirt.

This encounter has made Clare even more wary at pick-up time. Stacey recognises them, so if she were to emerge from the ominous white house at the same time that William walked through the school gates then she would spot him. What if she starts stalking him, causing him distress? These are more Clare's concerns than mine; Stacey is too chaotic and uncommitted to hassle him, and Jo says social services and the police are 'on to it'.

But I feel protective over him, wanting to avoid an unexpected encounter like this happening again. He's always known he's adopted, it's part of his everyday language – we even talk about the cats being adopted into our family. How much of it he can comprehend, we don't know, although it's been helpful to unpack more of it with him alongside adopting Hope, slowly and gently explaining his adoption in the context of hers. But until the other day he had no idea what Stacey looked like, having not seen his Life Story Book yet. So, this run-in with a strange lady calling him 'Graydon' unsettled him, sparking questions and making some of the theoretical concepts more concrete when Clare explained to him afterwards who she was; *this* is the tummy that he came from, *this* is his birth mother who couldn't keep him safe.

A few days later at bedtime William asked, "why did that lady, the one who's tummy I grew in, never find me to say sorry to me?" Saying sorry comes up frequently at the moment; the importance of which we reinforce daily, usually in the context of sibling disagreements. Somehow William knows that he has been wronged by Stacey. He senses, deep within him, that he deserves an apology for something, despite not being able to comprehend what that something is. I don't want him to carry the weight of being wronged, the bitterness and unforgiveness.

I look at him now, still sitting on my dad's knee, unusually still, watching his older cousins clearing the table and setting up a game of Uno. Clare and I are aware we're entering into unchartered territory as adoptive parents; coming up against questions and emotions that are hard to contain and explain. We want to be honest, never lying or underestimating what William can process, while responding wisely, knowing that there are things that are hard for his young mind to comprehend. We want to constantly reassure him that he's wanted, loved and safe. Stacey couldn't keep him safe, however much she wanted to, but we can.

Clare has disappeared into the kitchen, laden with dishes, followed by Rachel. I can hear the two of them talking, Rachel gently asking Clare if she's ok. Clare's saying she's worried about William and drowning in anxieties regarding Hope's adoption and what to do about Stacey's baby. I move away to give them space, joining my niblings in their game of Uno. I'm thinking back to when I noticed Clare sitting on the kitchen floor in tears yesterday, listening to the radio; 'You're gonna be ok, hope is never lost', the musician sang. I'm praying those timely words resonate with her.

My head's not in the game and I lose spectacularly, my niece Nancy serving me nearly all the 'pick up four' cards in the pack.

Perhaps something had shifted in Clare while she sat on the kitchen floor, or maybe she felt spurred on by the unanimous support from my family over Sunday lunch. Whatever the reason, on the sixth of December she somehow finds the courage to utter the three simple words that trigger our latest life tsunami: "Let's do it."

We ring Jo straight away and tell her. "We're in. We'll delay Hope's adoption and take the baby." She doesn't seem surprised, as if she knew Clare would ultimately come round to this choice. Following this call, we both take a breath and relax for an evening, watching television and not thinking, in recognition of all the over-thinking we've been doing recently.

On the seventh of December, Jo calls us back, "She's been born." Yikes; the sequence of events feels reminiscent of the speed at which things moved with William and Hope, and suddenly we're rushing around like headless chickens figuring out what we need to do to prepare for her arrival. But – surprise, surprise – there is a delay in the paperwork, which is yet to be sorted. We still need an interim care order to be granted for the baby, meaning that they will go straight into care. This order was already in place when we met William and Hope, but has been held up this time, I expect in part due to Stacey registering her pregnancy so late. Once the interim care order is in place we then need to be approved as foster carers for a second child. This buys us a bit more time, which we need, but also don't want. We're desperate to meet her; it feels like being held at arm's length from our own daughter.

On the eighth of December an interim care order is granted. This baby will definitely go into care when she's discharged from hospital, we just need the powers that be to decree that we can handle fostering two babies at once. We're also told that she's in NICU receiving treatment for neonatal abstinence syndrome and we are now beside ourselves with frustration that bureaucracy is holding us back from her.

When William was in NICU we were so aware of how stretched the staff were and how little he was held. I think back to the fake hand left on his chest for comfort, and then think of *this* little baby, alone in an incubator. We could be holding her now, if someone could just get round to signing the paperwork. We could have been holding her from day one of her life. It's infuriating that we're not and that the days are ticking by.

On the ninth of December we head to Mothercare to duplicate all our baby items and keep us distracted from our impatience and swelling frustration.

Hope is only ten months. She's still using her cot, her highchair, her buggy, and most of her other baby-related things. We need another one of everything, and to upgrade to a double buggy. Clare seems to have snapped into action, suddenly finding decision-making infinitely easier. We discuss how we're going to cope when the baby comes home with us. It's clear that Clare is at capacity a lot of the time with William and Hope. We agree that I'll take the baby to work with me as much as I can – provided she's not as distressed as William was in those early months.

Five agonising days pass with no progress. William keeps asking when 'Baby Jo' will deliver his next sister. Jo is now officially 'Baby Jo' in our household. As far as William is concerned this is where babies come from: Jo.

The fourteenth of December is Clare's birthday. The frivolities are a much-needed distraction. We tell William how Clare used to jokingly ask for a baby for her birthday, and then on her thirty-seventh birthday she got *him*! He doesn't quite follow, but enjoys our enthusiasm. And then the phone rings. It's Baby Jo. We've been approved as foster carers for another baby. "You can come in and meet her tomorrow."

And so, on the fifteenth of December, nine days after agreeing to foster another baby, Clare is in hospital meeting the newest member of our family.

One of us has to stay at home with Hope as we're not allowed to leave her with anyone else while we're in the fostering phase. So I'm sifting through a box of Christmas decorations with William and Hope in an attempt to distract ourselves – we're late getting them up this year, baby preparations talking precedence over Christmas.

I'm still daydreaming about some show-stopper Christmas display on the front of the house – lots of lights and an inflatable snowman – but yet to convince Clare it's worth the investment.

I'm waiting for Clare to ring with an update on how things are going. I feel a bit at a loss, waiting for news. I don't hear anything until lunchtime, hours after she left for the hospital.

Thankfully William and Hope are temporarily silenced by the vast amounts of food they're stuffing into their mouths – hamster style. At what point do children start eating less like animals?

"Oh Jeremy, she's so incredibly tiny," she says as soon as I answer the phone, without any 'hellos'. "Even tinier than Hope was. Only four pounds."

"How's she doing? How's her withdrawal?" Hope is banging her sippy-cup against her highchair and babbling loudly. I cover my other ear with my free hand.

"The doctor says she'll be ok. It's really hard to see her like this, Jeremy. She looks so alone, and apparently Stacey's been really disengaged."

"That doesn't surprise me... Have you seen her?"

"Yes. I saw her as she was leaving. She kept asking how Graydon is doing and Jo said I didn't need to answer that question and told Stacey that it wasn't her right to know anymore – in her kind, but firm Jo-like way. You know what I mean,"

I'm responding to cries of "more carroooot!" from William, while Clare continues, seemingly without taking a breath. "And she's said that Stacey now needs to come in in the afternoons, as we'll be there in the mornings. She's just so tiny, Jeremy. And still so early on with her withdrawal. She's so..."

"Tell me more when you get home," I interrupt, distracted by Hope, who is now making a slow waterfall onto the floor with the sippy-cup. When did lunch become such a stressful, multitasking affair? "When will you be back?"

"I'll stay as long as I can. Maybe home by three pm?"

That sounds optimistic to me. I tell her there's no need to rush back and I'm about to put the phone down when I remember. "Oh, Clare! Are you still there?"

"Yep?"

"I forgot to ask. What's her name?"

"Oh yes... about that... Stacey's named her... *Fierce*."

Two days later I get to meet her. We can't quite bring ourselves to call her Fierce. We've thought through all the positive connotations – how love can be fierce and protective, and how we can be fierce in our passions and in the way we fight for justice. At ten days old she's already a fighter, so in some ways it seems right. But looking at her now, so delicate and helpless, I can't call her Fierce. It seems that social services also have their reservations about how appropriate the name is, especially after Stacey has insinuated that for her it's more reflective of the anger she feels towards the world, wanting her daughter to fiercely reflect this hostility. Stacey's social worker is encouraging her to register Fierce by her middle name, Emily, instead. Most of the hospital staff are calling her 'little fighter', or baby Fi.

She's back in NICU receiving antibiotics for a rash she developed the other day. There's an intravenous line coming out of her tiny hand, strapped to her arm to keep it in place. She's fast asleep and I'm relishing being alone with her, studying her face and soaking her in. Her top lip is protruding a little, like the beak of a baby bird, and she has a little dimple on her chin. I'm surprised by how peaceful she is in my arms. We had plenty of peaceful moments with Hope and William as babies once they were through their withdrawal, but I seem to have been left with resounding memories of them in distress, reeling with discomfort. It feels unusual to be holding her, so still, no rocking or swaddling or soothing shushing needed right now. I feel so deeply assured that we made the right choice. In fact, it feels ludicrous that there was ever a choice to make. To love her and protect her now isn't a choice but a natural instinct. She is instinctively ours.

William has been able to meet baby Fi, seeing as he's her biological half-sibling. Clare said he was so gentle with her, speaking softly and genuinely delighting in meeting another tiny sister. But we haven't been allowed to bring Hope in, and Clare and I are both feeling a deep, almost urgent, need to be all together. We're creeping closer to the twenty-fifth, and Clare can't stop saying how much she wants Fi home for Christmas. I want the same, I'm just voicing it less, pretending to be very measured and pragmatic about the situation.

In truth, I'm not feeling realistic at all. I'm even contemplating still going to the in-laws in Petersfield for Christmas day, staying in a Premier Inn round the corner as planned, with an energetic four-year-old, a nine-month-old in what seems to be a continual sleep regression, and a two-week-old with neonatal abstinence syndrome. But this is unlikely to happen, I tell myself, after thinking through all the logistics. Something is bound to go wrong with the paperwork and she will have to stay in longer.

But the bonkers plan ends up playing out when we get a call from the hospital on the twenty-first to say that she will be discharged *tomorrow.* We're on! We'll have one full day at home as a family of five and then head to Petersfield on the twenty-fourth.

On the twenty-second I wait on standby at home with William and Hope for a call from Clare to say we can pick up her and baby Fi up from the hospital. I'm glad that we can collect her this time and don't have to await a delivery as we did with Hope. We hear nothing for most of the day – by nothing, I mean no actual information, just selfies of Clare with baby Fi. I imagine the discharge procedure is taking a while, and Stacey should be coming in to say goodbye, although she's only been back to the hospital a few times since giving birth, so we're not sure what to expect.

At three pm we finally get the call saying she's about to be discharged. I immediately bundle Hope and William into the car and set off. En route, Clare calls to say that baby Fi doesn't have any clothes. "What about the ones she's been wearing the last few weeks?" I ask, trying hard not to sound indignant. "They're *fine*. Surprisingly tasteful for Stacey, actually."

"Well, that's the thing," Clare explains. "Stacey didn't buy them, apparently they belong to the hospital and they need to keep hold of them, so baby Fi will be coming home naked unless you can swing by somewhere and get her some clothes."

So we do, William and Hope hampering my productivity every step of the way, as Hope tries to wriggle out my arms and William attempts to hang off the side of the shopping basket. But once in the right aisle, William helps me choose a snowman onesie to go over some basic baby grows, and I spontaneously buy matching sparkly navy blue dresses for Hope and Fi to wear on Christmas day.

We bring baby Fi home, swamped in a newborn snowman onesie, far too big for a baby weighing only four pounds. Clare, giddy with the thrill of it all – "Fi is home! And it's only two days till Christmas!" –

declares that our annual elf picture will be taking place "prompto!" We dutifully get into our costumes – the newborn elf outfit that William once wore having been dug out of the cupboard – and adorn our smiles, which are usually fake and tongue in cheek, but this year entirely authentic.

Two days later we're on the road to Mike and Shirley's in Petersfield, with three car seats wedged in the back. William is pressing buttons willy nilly in a Thomas the Tank Engine noisy book, but he is ultimately engaged so I can tolerate the repetitive sounds of train horns, and miraculously, both Hope and baby Fi are asleep. I imagine this doesn't bode well for bedtime, but I'm relishing the relative peace and an opportunity for a snatched conversation with Clare.

I'm not sure what I expected to feel, but right now, we're exhilarated. And despite the fact that everything we're doing is entirely legitimate – everything other than taking baby Fi on holiday, which technically we shouldn't be doing until her placement order is issued, but we're ninety percent sure social services will turn a blind eye to this because it's Christmas – it feels like we've pulled off an impressive heist. We're driving into the distance with our *three children* in the back. I never thought this day would come.

Christmas rolls by in an intense, overwhelming blur.

I have no time to reflect on whether I'm actually enjoying it or not. I may well be, but I'm fully employed in responding to the infinite needs of my little family: changing nappies; rocking baby Fi, who turns out to be more distressed by her withdrawal than we'd anticipated; trailing Hope who has decided to start crawling at this opportune moment and is a complete liability with all Shirley's ornaments (of which there are many); and trying to make sure

William feels seen and valued amidst the chaos of all the loud electronic toys his kind relatives have bestowed on him.

We're all in one room together in the Premier Inn. We enquire about a second room, not having expected to bring a newborn on our Christmas holiday, but are told there's 'no room in the inn'. So we squeeze in together and grin and bear it.

Boiling kettles to warm bottles in the middle of the night while trying not to disturb William and Hope.

Needless to say, none of us get much sleep, and by the time we're driving home to see my family on Boxing Day we're barely functioning. It sets the tone for what's ahead – a season fuelled by sheer determination and willpower.

We're 'living our dream' but barely able to notice, consumed by the daily needs of our three small humans.

Come the new year, I wrap Fi in a sling on my front and take her to work. She's cocooned and calm, the gentle rise and fall of my chest soothing her. I text Clare when she needs a bottle and then feed her on my lap, my camera high enough that she's out of shot in video calls with clients. She seems to have settled into her body, no longer disturbed by pain and discomfort; the drugs she was dependent on in the womb no longer laying hold of her.

She's still unsettled at times, as all babies are, but we can meet her needs and calm her. It's empowering and reassuring, significantly easier at times then trying to navigate the complex emotional needs of a four-year-old or the physical demands of a mobile, destructive eleven-month-old.

We're told by Jo that Stacey has registered Fi's birth and that she's now officially... Fierce. It doesn't surprise me that she's defied social services advice, perhaps I would have done the same in her situation – asserting power where I can when the rest of life is out of control. But the general agreement among the social workers is that Fierce is not an appropriate name and that they would support her name being changed if adopted.

They are now referring to her as Emily. While it feels strange to change her name after a few weeks of calling her Fi, we're relieved, and love the name Emily. We pray she'll be someone who loves fiercely – as we imagine Stacey would have, had her life circumstances been different – but that any fierce passion she feels won't fuel anger and bitterness towards the world.

The looming question remains as to who Emily's birth father is. Stacey has given a list of seventeen potential names which social services have helped her narrow down to two; one is a known paedophile, the other a member of a local gang. Her hunch is currently with the local gang member – whose Mediterranean heritage would explain Emily's olive complexion. But, not unexpectedly, he refuses to cooperate for a DNA test, and when his mother offers to give a hair sample he threatens to kill her. So, with death threats flying around, the hunt for a birth father comes to an abrupt halt.

Initially, Stacey turns up to contact sessions. When I hand Emily over I wonder why the contact supervisor is cold towards me, as if I'm the perpetrator, a baby stealer. But I'm not ruffled or perturbed. On the contrary, I'm almost pleased that after hours of observing Stacey with Emily, the supervisor feels compassion. She must see Stacey's love, beneath her bravado and seeming disconnection. Perhaps being aloof masks her distress. There is so much we could accuse Stacey of – she's been infuriatingly irresponsible – but we're also aware she would care for William and Emily if she could. She has agency, but she's also trapped in a lifestyle that was dictated by an upbringing where love was thin and anger and destructive behaviour the norm.

She makes some attempts to fight for Emily – I'm glad she does, and I want Emily to know this – requesting a parenting assessment on the off chance that she's deemed able to care for Emily at a parent and baby unit. But as the weeks progress, she seems to be so lost or trapped in the day-to-day of her addictions that she loses track, and never even turns up to the parenting assessment that her social worker goes to great lengths to secure for her.

The two-day hearing to discuss a placement order for Emily turns into a simple two *hour* hearing when Stacey's solicitor reads out a letter from Stacey explaining that she is not in a place to 'fight for Emily', despite wanting to. It's a simple win for us – Emily is now officially up for adoption – with the uncomfortable backdrop of Stacey's life unravelling. She's losing her fight, giving in to the current that's sweeping her further into controlling relationships and relentless waves of drink and drugs.

We celebrate getting the placement order gently; holding the joy of being one step closer to Emily being ours alongside Stacey's loss.

Amidst all this, Hope's adoption goes through. I'm moved by the hordes of friends and family who respond to our invitation and gather en masse for her celebration hearing; so many, the judge has to conduct the hearing in the main courtroom to accommodate us all. The grandeur of the venue is indicative of the magnitude of the moment. We've arrived. She's *ours!* Our collective joy is tangible, the room buzzing with elation and a profound sense of satisfaction and completion, akin to having crossed the finish line after competing in an extreme endurance sport.

As I stand at the front during the formal part of the hearing, I can't help but think of how Tegan and Nate would have been here in this very room when their worlds imploded; when the judge pronounced his judgement and permanently removed Hope from their care. They lost her in this room, and here we are in the same room, gaining her. I acknowledge this reflection, feeling acutely the proximity of loss and gain for a moment, but leave it in the wings and let the joy of Hope being ours forever – Hope *Wilson* – take centre stage.

We've squeezed back into the outfits we wore for William's celebration hearing a few years ago, aiming to replicate a family picture, this time with two new additions. As we pose for the picture William steals the judge's wig – the same judge who presided at his own celebration hearing – and sits in his chair, pretending to conduct the proceedings. The judge laughs at William's antics and seems touched, perhaps overwhelmed, by how the hearing is unfolding, commenting that he's never experienced celebration hearings like William's and Hope's – the energy and joy, "you know how to celebrate!" he laughs, and we feel honoured to have journeyed with friends and family who want to cheer us on with such fervour.

Our friends John and Penny offer to pray for us again, and I swell with gratitude for the gift of faith in a God who has gently sustained us through so much. I don't take it for granted, and it feels apt that we all head straight from the courtroom to our friends' church for a dedication service for Hope.

"You know every step I will take before my journey even begins," Clare's dad reads from Psalm 139 of the Passion translation of the Bible during the service. "You've gone into my future to prepare the way and in kindness you follow behind me to spare me from the harm of my past. You have laid your hand on me. This is just too wonderful, deep and incomprehensible." I turn to look at Hope – my *daughter* – as Mike reads these words of incomprehensible beauty; words that talk of being intimately known, loved and held by God.

This day feels perfect in so many ways, despite the logistics of herding everyone from Taunton, across the hills, to a tiny village church that Google Maps seems unable to find, and then squeezing them all into the pews. Our celebrating is wholehearted and untethered. But throughout the day Emily comes in and out of my arms, and every time I hold her I ache. She is our missing piece of the puzzle. The one who makes our family whole. But she's not yet wholly ours, and I feel unable to rest until she is.

As the months pass, Emily's adoption slows down. Jo submits paperwork to the court after our matching panel is successful, but hears nothing, eventually discovering that it was somehow lost.

Stacey is also lost, with her social worker unable to track her down. Missing paperwork and missing people leaving us in limbo. Summer passes and we're into autumn, with William starting school, Hope toddling around shouting 'where you Weeeeam?!' in his absence, and Emily chasing Hope on all fours. We seem to live in a permanent state of chaos, occasionally glimpsing sanity when Emily sleeps through the night (beating Hope to it) and William settles into his reception class.

Meanwhile, we carry the weight of the ongoing adoption process in our bodies – adrenaline constantly pulsing in our veins, low level anxiety keeping our heart rates up. We're ready to be alone – just Wilsons – free from the system, free from the perpetual dramas and uncertainties. Jo retires and we lament her absence. We feel so close to the end and yet can't quite see it on the horizon. We wish she was still alongside us, giving us that strength to get over the finish line.

As autumn turns to winter and Emily's first birthday comes and goes, we find out that Stacey wasn't lost, but rather behind bars after assaulting a police officer. She hasn't seen Emily for over six months, but still decides to contest the adoption from prison – despite having previously sent the letter saying she wouldn't be fighting for her – delaying the process still further and significantly tampering with our emotions. If the judge were to agree to support her challenge – which is very unlikely, but not impossible – then this would delay the process for an *entire year* while Stacey serves her sentence. We are incredulous, our compassion for her temporarily waning. What good could this possibly do?

This year I rig Christmas lights onto the front of the house for the first time. Finally, my vision is coming to fruition.

I start with the more tasteful elements to ease Clare in; next year will see the addition of a giant inflatable snowman. She's going to love it. We all gather together on the front lawn for the grand turning on of the Wilson Christmas lights. William is pretending he has 'light power'– we roll with this and Clare hits 'on' just as he throws out his little arms towards the house, fingers spread, surging with power. He's amazed by his own power, as are Hope and Emily, as the house lights up, dazzling our neighbours, and bringing joy to yet another Christmas spent in uncertainty.

I'm surprised by the turnout. Some ten to fifteen people gathered in the Costa Coffee in Taunton, cupping their hot chocolates and smoothies, waiting quietly for the event to start. It's a good venue, better than the nondescript, soulless village hall we went to years ago when we started out on this journey. It's also a beautiful spring evening – the clocks changed a few weeks ago and we're enjoying longer, warmer days, making everything feel more optimistic.

After a brief welcome, Anusha from Somerset County Council glances in my direction as if to give me prior warning that I'm up next.

"Without further ado, let me introduce you to *Jeremy* who is here to share his journey through Fostering for Adoption with you. He and his wife Clare are the first couple in the country to successfully adopt *three times* through the Fostering for Adoption initiative," she looks at me beaming, while I squirm internally. 'Successfully' strikes me as a strange word to use, suggesting that we're somehow professionals in this adoption approach that has been wildly out of our control, and subject to so many external factors. It also jars with the fact that our 'success' was someone else's loss. I wonder how I can gently make these points during my allotted time, without making Anusha feel uncomfortable. In the meantime, I smile and look around at all the impressed and curious faces.

I tell our story from the beginning, trying to condense the roller coaster ride of the last five years into twenty minutes. I feel unexpectedly emotional towards the end as I explain the agonising delays of the last few months; how beholden our lives have been to slow paper work and other people's errors, and how Stacey contested Emily's adoption right at the last moment.

"But Emily was officially adopted a month ago," I conclude, with a few of the group bursting into spontaneous applause as I say this. Their response feels apt, and I soak in the relief of finally being able to say this. "Congratulations!" one woman calls out, and I thank her, unable to help myself from grinning widely and soaking in their vicarious pleasure. Emily's celebration hearing was just a couple of days ago and I'm still almost breathless with the joy of it; the same amazing crowd of people gathered together in the same courtroom, marking the momentous moment.

Just as I'm about to sit down a man on the front row raises a hand. "Oh, a question!" Anusha exclaims, clearly delighted by the level of engagement. "I'm sure Jeremy would be happy to take questions," she says, looking from him to me. Lucky for her I am.

"Go ahead!" I say to the man in the front row.

"This has clearly all turned out very well for you..." he says. I nod in agreement, wondering where this is going. "But it sounds like one hell of a journey. So I'm intrigued..." he pauses.

So am I, what is he going to ask?

"Would you do it again?"

PART 3

2022–2023

CHAPTER 15 – Five till seven

January 2022

Jeremy

Emily is looking up at me, her clothes dishevelled and twigs sticking out of her thin, mousy-brown, shoulder-length hair. A wide grin is spread across her face, her freckled nose wrinkled, and her eyes squeezed half closed. She's holding something behind her back. What's she up to? I add some chicken to the frying pan, continuing my cooking and waiting to see how this plays out. She keeps me on my toes; a handful one moment and helpful the next. She's sparky and surprising – a bit like Clare. It's hard to believe that she'll be starting school in September this year. I can still feel the sensation of her wrapped in the sling on my front as a newborn.

It's been nearly three years since her adoption; three years since we all became Wilsons, living a step removed from the insecurities and suspense that characterised life for so long. The Covid pandemic hit us a year after Emily's adoption, launching us into a different kind of anxious season, but the drama, although affecting us, was happening around us. We, the Wilsons, in our home in rural Somerset, were ok. While the world moved into a state of uncertainty, we finally embraced a life of assurance for the first time in years, without social services guiding or dictating our next move. Naturally it was chaos at times – Emily and Hope potty training at the same time; William being assessed for ADHD over videocall; Clare and I juggling work and parenting in every waking hour – but it was *our* chaos to mould and respond to.

I've made the decision to carry on cooking dinner and ignore Emily's antics, but she's now giggling in a 'look at me, Daddy' sort of way, shuffling around the kitchen to block my path from the hob to the spice rack in a bid get my attention.

"Emily!" I say, pretending I hadn't seen her. "What are you up to? Would you like to help me cook Mummy's dinner?" She doesn't answer, but raises her eyebrows and continues to giggle. What's she got behind her back? Knowing Emily, it could be anything. A dead mouse Coben's bought in that she's decided to adopt? Or another worm to add to her little collection? Although she knows she's not meant to bring the worms inside.

Our exchange is interrupted by Hope, now nearly five, hollering, "MR BOTTOM INSPECTOR!" at the top of her lungs. That's me. Clearly my services are required in the bathroom. Some recent slap-dash bottom wiping from Hope has seen me promoted to Mr Bottom Inspector. What a glamorous life I lead.

I abandon my curry-prep to address the bottom – which thankfully needs no further attention on this occasion – and I'm turning my focus back to a shifty looking Emily when William, now eight, appears at the top of the stairs chanting, "bottom, bottom!" and wiggling his bottom around. This will infuriate Hope no end; William knows just how to wind her up while simultaneously knowing exactly how to make Emily laugh.

William keeps chanting; Emily descends into uncontrollable giggles at the mention of bottoms; Hope starts pursing her lips and flaring her nostrils. I need to defuse the situation, fast, but my brain seems unable to move quick enough to come up with an effective, creative solution. This could turn into a full-on brawl in a minute! I don't know if I've got the energy to deal with the inevitable direction this is going in.

I succumbed to Covid a few months ago, despite having had my vaccinations, and ended up being hospitalised – dramatically collapsing in the entrance to A&E, needing resuscitating and teetering on the edge of life and death for a week in the Covid intensive care ward. As if we needed more drama in our life. I'm nearly back to full health now, and we've rolled into the new year and new term with fresh optimism. But at this time of day I feel the bone-heavy tiredness slowly claiming me. Bedtime feels a long way off.

Clare appears behind William at the top of the stairs, surveying the situation. She starts asking William to stop saying bottom when Hope chimes in with, "The next person to say *bottom* is a stinky poo!" This immediately mutes William, but Emily – hyped up by the situation and laughing so hard she hasn't heard what Hope's said – bellows, "BOTTOM!" at the top of her lungs, cueing melodic chants of "You're a stinky poo!" from William and Hope. In a split-second Emily's wild exhilaration has transformed into rage. She resembles a wolf with its hackles up. William and Hope, like prey sensing danger, run squealing into the living room with Emily in hot pursuit. This has all gone down in a matter of seconds; one moment I was cooking a curry, about to pour myself an early evening G&T, the next moment I'm witnessing a ferocious showdown. My sleep-deprived brain can barely keep up.

I follow them into the living room – yelling, "Clare, give the chicken a stir!" over my shoulder – in time to witness Emily launch herself at William, claws out, teeth bared. "Right!" I attempt to keep my tone light and friendly in a bid to tame my unruly brood and not escalate the situation. "Emily, you are *not* a stinky poo," I confirm, peeling her off William before she does any damage. "Hope and William, please *stop*!"

It doesn't take long to calm the girls. Emily has a little cry and a cuddle on my lap, lamenting the distress of being labelled a stinky poo, while Hope is easily distracted by a book about Blaze and the Monster Machines, her current obsession. William, meanwhile, is escalating. I feel momentarily frustrated with myself for not spotting this sooner, helping him to stay calm and connected. I'd noticed him starting to get agitated at dinner, Emily's incessant tapping on the table triggering his frustration. I wonder what it's like for him? I also found her tapping irritating, but I know it's at another level for William, as if the uncontrollable tapping is taking place inside his head. He was already tired, the Christmas season having been especially overstimulating and the start of term requiring extra concentration and emotional energy; this latest wild exchange seems to have tipped him over the edge. Once his little brain gets going – overloaded and stimulated, unable to keep up with regular, day-to-day processing demands – it's really hard to bring him back. It's a fight or flight state.

I gently tease the twig out of Emily's hair, watching William and Clare out the corner of my eye. He keeps switching between holding his head and bashing a pillow with his fist. Clare's sitting on the arm of the couch, having abandoned the chicken-stirring, asking softly if she can give him a hug. He's saying, "you don't love me. I'm *stupid,*" on repeat. To which Clare replies, "I love you. You're wonderful. I'm just going to wait here."

I'm full of admiration for her in this moment. It's so hard to stay calm, especially when we're all tired after Christmas and new year, and still emotionally drained from processing my near brush with death, which I think Clare's only finding the headspace to process now that I'm better and the kids are back at school and pre-school.

She went into adrenaline-fuelled survival mode for a few months, burning through her last reserves. It's so tempting in these moments, when our own energy levels are so low, to just shout for William to "snap out of it", and to "stop being silly"; to remove the pillow, or whatever it is he's bashing, and succumb to frustration. It's so tempting to try and control the situation, when what he needs is our steady, calm presence to hold him through it.

Some situations are harder than others, especially the ones that feel more personal. A few days ago he was so upset in the car that he started shouting, "I don't want to be here!" and, "I don't want you to be my mum!" at Clare. We know he doesn't mean it. We try to hold the words lightly, but they are so painful to hear. William *could* have had different parents, someone else *could* have stepped forward or been matched with him. I don't tend to dwell on this, but I know Clare does, periodically needing reminding that however numerous the could-have-beens, we're *it.* The only parents for him; the *right* parents for him. We trust this and lean into it, but in that moment Clare was so upset that her distress manifested as anger. Later on, she berated herself further for not having been able to find a place to park her emotions, when she'd desperately needed to find space to contain his. It's complex, this parenting business; our emotions matter, we get angry too, but we must find the emotional capacity to make sure William, Hope and Emily feel safe. We fervently want them to feel safe, whether they're kind to us or not.

Right now, Clare has somehow contained the frustration and exhaustion I know she feels and is all empathy; sitting, waiting, and repeating her consistent mantra to William: "I love you. You're wonderful. I'm just going to wait here."

We want to see the world from William's perspective, adjusting our expectations, re-learning how we think things *should* be whilst empowering him to meet us somewhere on that journey. Our world is set up for a neurotypical brain, and Clare and I have been left wondering how we can change the things within our sphere of influence, learning from and accommodating a busier, overactive brain like William's. Since William was officially diagnosed with ADHD in the summer of 2020 we've had more insight and empathy. We want to equip him to live in a neurotypical world, to cope with the stimulating environments he's constantly exposed to, but we also want to give him space for his beautiful, electric mind to be free, for his energy to be enjoyed, and his way of absorbing and reacting to the world to be something we learn from.

But right now, his busy mind doesn't feel beautiful to him. It's a burden and he's cross with himself. It's painful to witness and hard to know how we could have nudged the sequence of events in a different direction. I wonder if anyone feels like they're really excelling as a parent, or whether we all feel like we're floundering... Maybe it's just us.

Emily has recovered from being called a stinky poo, but is feeling increasingly riled by William, who is now saying 'chicken wings' over and over again. "Chicken wings. Chicken wings. Chicken wings."

"Make him stop!" she shouts. "Agh, *William*!"

I try to explain to her that he can't help it – he sometimes has these Tourette's -like symptoms, when he latches on to a word or phrase that feels good to say and repeats it in an attempt to self-regulate. In lockdown it was 'Boris Johnson' over and over again, so 'Chicken wings' is an improvement. I try to extract Emily and Hope from the living room, but Emily's irritation has already been absorbed by William, who is now flailing his arms in her direction. I don't think he means to hit her, but I'm not quick enough to block his arms before they connect with her legs. She's now screaming, "*naughty* William!" while Clare attempts to gently restrain him, moving him through to the utility room off the lounge. She's countering Emily's comments with, "You're *not* naughty William, but I am going to need to remove you so Emily doesn't get hurt."

I find myself thinking back to the first adoption information evening we went to, when a father spoke about his child's behaviour. He went to great lengths to emphasise that their scratching, screaming and emotional meltdowns weren't 'bad'. I'd found it confusing at the time, having been exposed to a more authoritarian style of parenting as a child; this was all I knew, and there was certainly a time when I would have observed William's behaviour right now and been alarmed, feeling a compulsion to shut the behaviour down without recognising its roots.

Having a 'naughty step' or 'time-out corner' has been tempting in moments when everything feels out of control, or our ability to respond is hampered by tiredness, but we never want the children to feel alone or rejected in their distress, even if it is self-inflicted. He's not bad, and he's not alone – it's paramount to us that he knows this, and the girls too. Even more so because they're adopted. We need them to know how *wanted* they are; that they weren't rejected or abandoned, that so many factors contributed to the story that unfolded; the story that meant they weren't safe with their birth parents, but are safe with us. We need them to know how safe they are.

So I know Clare will sit with William until he's calmed down. Often it's a surprise that snaps him out of his chaotic cycle of thoughts, like a sudden one-off loud noise. It can be hard to predict. One evening, last week, when he was lost in a hyped state, he started seeing spiders everywhere – occasional hallucinations are a side effect of his ADHD medication – and we ended up coaxing him into the shower to startle him out of his confusion and distress. I went in with him, both fully clothed, holding him and reminding him that he's safe and loved, letting the water run over us, restoring calm.

Back in the kitchen I momentarily wonder if I can salvage the burnt chicken, but decide to abandon it for now and get the girls in the bath. Maybe they all need an early bedtime. I know I do. Emily is distracted by something en route, resuming her suspicious behaviour from earlier. I don't have much energy for games right now, so instead of playing along I go for the direct approach and ask her what's behind her back.

Hope interrupts, "It's a phone. She's got a *phone*."

A phone? Emily sticks her tongue out at Hope, revealing a phone in a pink, sparkly case from behind her back. I don't recognise it. "It's Julie's," Hope continues. Julie is one of Emily's pre-school teachers.

"It's really sparkly and beautiful," Emily adds, stroking the back of it. She must have a vague sense of having done something she shouldn't, otherwise she wouldn't have been hiding it behind her back. But right now she seems blissfully unaware of the consequences of having essentially stolen her teacher's phone just because it was pretty.

I'm liable to blow a fuse at my little magpie-eyed pickpocket but, unexpectedly, tiredness works in my favour. Too exhausted to respond right now, I take a deep breath and other than saying, "I'll call school and let Julie know we're looking after her phone until tomorrow," and, "It's never ok to take something that belongs to someone else," I leave the topic till later – one to thrash through with Clare to find a united way forward.

But it plagues me, as I sit watching the girls playing with Clare's rubber duck collection in the bath. Surely Emily knows she can't take things? But she seems unable to help herself sometimes. When we were in a restaurant having brunch a few weeks ago, she went to the toilets with Clare and on her way back picked up some keys dangling out of someone's bag. We had to go around asking if anyone had lost their keys to identify where they came from and return them to their rightful owner. I need to remind myself that she's only just turned four – still exploring and pushing boundaries. I imagine it's fairly normal behaviour. But it's also hard to determine, with very little to compare it to. Is it all down to development and boundary pushing? What aspects of their behaviours and character come from their birth parents? What things have we intentionally or inadvertently nurtured? Will we ever know? And does it matter?

I sit with my questions, looking at these two unique little humans squirting water from rubber ducks into each other's faces. I know them so deeply – held them and loved them from weeks old; I know their characters and their quirks, their heartaches and their joys – and yet they're mysteries to me. As Clare is also; known, yet a mystery. As I am to myself. As I imagine any human would be, whether they came from me or not.

"This baby duck came from this one," Emily says, pairing a baby rubber duck up with the batman duck.

"And this one's adopted by this funny clown duck," Hope laughs. "Hello ducky ducky duck duck!"

"Which tummy did it come from?" Emily asks, picking up Hope's baby duck.

"It didn't come from a tummy, *silly*," Hope rolls her eyes, "Ducks lay EGGS!"

"I know THAT!" Emily shouts, squirting Hope with water from the batman duck. She'd clearly forgotten. "I think *this* ducky laid the egg *that* baby came from." She picks up the Queen Elizabeth duck. "A princess baby duck."

There's a pause while the ducks quack around for a minute, and I'm wondering whether to try and do something productive while this game is taking place, when Hope turns to me and asks, "which tummy did I come from again?"

She's caught me off guard. "This one!" I say, picking up the Taylor Swift duck.

She laughs, but knocks it out my hand, "no, *really,*" she insists. "I came from a different tummy from William and Emily, didn't I?"

"Yes. You grew inside a lady called Tegan," I keep my tone as light as I can, but I watch Hope carefully. She's focused on her ducks.

"Yes, Tegan," she repeats. "Tegan... This one's called Tegan," she says, picking up the Queen Elizabeth duck again and swimming it towards her baby duck.

Clare appears in the doorway. "Can we switch?" She looks drained. "William's calm now. He'd like to read books with you."

I give her a hug on my way past. "You managed that so well," I whisper. "Oh, and heads up," I add, "they're playing mummies and babies with the ducks, and that one," I nod at the Queen Elizabeth one, "is called *Tegan*."

William's curled up on the sofa looking at a Pokémon book. "Dad," he says not looking up, "did you know that the boy Pokémons have flat tails and the girl Pokémons have heart shaped tails?"

"No I didn't!" Pokémon is a baffling world. "Can you tell me about this one?" I ask, sitting down next to him and pointing at a Pokémon that looks like a whale, and listening as he expertly explains its powers and defences. I wonder whether I could help him understand himself in terms of powers and defences? Something to ponder.

"How was school today?" I ask, hoping that catching him relaxed and unawares may elicit more than the shrug I received in response to this question earlier.

"Mrs Everett said she loved the sketch book I brought in for show and tell. She especially loved my dragon drawing," he smiles, blushing a little. He's pleased with himself and I love witnessing him experiencing this emotion.

"I'm sure she did," I say, putting my arm round him and drawing him close.

When William received his ADHD diagnosis, an EHCP was put in place. I'm confident that it will be helpful in the future, but the County Council's first attempt at a plan felt token – complete with the wrong pronouns, and even the wrong child's name at one point in the document. We had to point out that this plan was meant to be for *William*, not Evie, and that simply changing names doesn't constitute a personally tailored plan. But EHCP or no EHCP, it's been his class teacher, Mrs Everett, and Mrs Webber, the school SENCO (Special Educational Needs Coordinator) who have transformed William's experience of school, understanding him and enabling him to feel safe and flourish.

"Can you read this now?" he asks, putting his Pokémon book to one side and plonking his Life Story Book on my lap, the one social services made for him to help him understand his adoption. He's in a phase of wanting to read it every night. Clare's taken the content and made it more child friendly – inspired by the one Hope's social worker made – complete with pictures of power rangers and a laminated front cover.

"William, you were born on Friday the twenty-second of November 2013," I read slowly, stroking his head. "You were born five weeks early by natural delivery. You weighed five pounds and five ounces, and you were forty-seven centimetres long. You needed to stay in the neonatal intensive care unit at hospital for twenty-one days." I pause for a moment, looking at the picture of William as a baby, recalling the moment when Clare placed him in my arms – finally I held him; *my child.* It was the most stilling and moving moment of my life.

I begin to turn the page but William puts his hand out to stop me. "No!" he says with force, "we skip past *that* page, remember?" It's the page with pictures of Stacey and Craig. Seeing their faces seems to make him angry. Understandably, he can't express why, and we've opted simply for skipping the page for now and not talking about it. We'll need to find a way of helping him address this anger one day. Or perhaps this anger is a necessary part of the grief cycle he'll face as he encounters emotions, moving through them and out the other side.

If I'm honest, I don't particularly like looking at that page either. I can manage it, but I could also do without it. We'll forever be inextricably linked with these individuals. We're no longer enmeshed with social services, but we'll never fully disentangle ourselves from Stacey, Craig, Tegan and Nate. They're part of our children's stories – part of *our* story. They crop up from time to time, as ducks in a game, or as pictures in a book. Clare even received a call the other day from a pharmacist asking to speak to Stacey about William's prescription. She's there, somewhere in his medical history, and misread information can easily lead to confusion. Clare had to explain that *she* is his mum, not Stacey, and request that the pharmacist go back and read his medical history carefully.

I read on, skipping the picture with Stacey and Craig, and the bit about their lives and why they couldn't keep him safe, until we get to pictures of our wider family – William's familiar world. He enjoys pointing out Grandad Bill and Grandma Pat, and seeing cousin Ross hold him as a baby, and the pictures of his adoption day. I read this book so often that I don't tend to give it much thought, but right now it's stirring up a lot of memories; the joy, the intensity, the uncertainty.

The other day Clare asked me if I'd do it again. "What if social services called tomorrow and said that Stacey was pregnant again," she'd said, "what would you do?"

I know she's fishing for a particular answer. I know she'd do it all again; take on the anxiety, elation and drama in order to bring hope and safety to another child's life, and more joy and chaos to ours. Her scenario is hypothetical, but it's not impossible. If social services called tomorrow, what would I say?

CHAPTER 16 – Sink or swim

November 2022 – ten months later

Clare

Dead? She's *dead*? I scroll down, checking I've got this right. I have.

"Look at this, Mummy!" Hope shouts. I don't move, still staring at my phone. Dead?!

"*Mummy*!" I look up. Hope's peeping over the side of the pool, her special prescription goggles on, checking I'm watching before she turns, pushing off from the side of the pool and wriggling like a fish under the water. She pops up halfway down the teaching pool, grinning, her little toes just able to touch the bottom, her face framed with water. I grin back and give her two enthusiastic thumbs up before gesturing in the direction of her teacher. Why is it always my kids who seem to be swimming in the opposite direction to everyone else in the class? She swims back to the rest of the group waiting at the edge for their next instruction, tucking herself in next to Emily, physically elbowing another child out the way. And why do my kids seem to be noticeably more boisterous?!

It's always loud in here with two classes going on at the same time – teachers projecting their voices, parents chatting away on benches lining the poolside, children yelling for their parents to stop chatting and watch – but today the echo is reverberating in my head. I search for William in the main pool, wondering how he's coping with the noise. He's on the edge of the group, currently looking up at the reflective glass ceiling rather than looking at his teacher, but seems to be calm and participating to some degree. I fish some paracetamol from my bag and gulp them down with a swig of water in an attempt to subdue my pounding headache.

I light the screen on my phone again. She looks back at me; pale skin, dark hair pulled into a slick high ponytail, wide smile and narrow, penetrating eyes. My throat feels tight. I want to call Jeremy, but he wouldn't be able to hear me if I called from in here, and I can't leave. I'm not sure if he can handle more bad news at the moment. His dad has been diagnosed with pancreatic cancer and is deteriorating fast, and his mum has recently been experiencing pain in her bones and we're worried the breast cancer she'd recently had the 'all clear' from may have spread. She's due a full body scan soon. I'm worried. We're stalked by loss.

I look back at Hope who is now at the other end of the pool doing some sort of victory dance. Maybe she just managed the full length?! I missed it! *Clare!* I seem to house a constant internal tension; desperately needing my own headspace and plotting how to be alone, whilst not wanting to miss a moment of their lives, wanting to rejoice in every sense of achievement, and lament with every sadness. They're changing so fast. I want to relish it, to soak in these incredible little souls I'm privileged to call mine, but I'm also exhausted and want the day to end so they can go to bed and I can sit alone with Jeremy and an uninterrupted meal.

I put my phone away, watching Hope intently, but aware that my mind is elsewhere. She's dead? Why on earth did social services not tell us?!

"Aw, she looks so like you, doesn't she!" The voice next to me makes me jump.

"Who? Oh, er, Hope? Well, er..." I never know to respond when people say this. Jeremy and I think they look nothing like us. I guess if you were to pick one of the three who looks most like me it would be Hope – similar sort of pale skin tone perhaps? Whereas Emily tans easily – never my forte. We've wondered whether the kids have picked up on our facial expressions over the years, mimicking them. Clearly people see *something.* I like that. But I'm yet to be well versed in my response.

"I guess she does a little bit," I confirm, adding, "she's adopted, so..."

"Oh *wow*. Ooh! Well, it's so great that she looks like you!" The woman replies. I've clearly made her feel awkward. She tucks her well-styled hair behind her ears. Makeup; hair clearly washed and blow-dried; nails painted; a coordinated outfit, carefully selected. Who is this breed of calm, collected, well-presented mum? I marvel. I miss fashion. Maybe I should ask Jeremy to get me those knee-high red boots I'm coveting for Christmas...

"You're very well matched with her," she adds, as if having a look-alike child was the goal. Concluding with, "What a *lovely* thing to do." I nod. *Lovely.* Would we call it *lovely*? There are many a word I'd use to describe adoption – overwhelming, brutal, glorious, life-changing, agonising – *lovely?*

I don't know where to go next with this conversation, so opt for, "Which one's yours?"

"Clementine," she points in the direction of a girl in Hope and Emily's class – the one Hope elbowed out the way. "*Clem,*" she clarifies, smiling sweetly and giving her daughter a little wave. I've noticed Clem in the changing rooms before, quietly getting changed and carefully folding her clothes away. We've ended up avoiding the changing rooms altogether recently as post-swimming antics were getting out of hand. I bundle the kids straight in the car in their bathrobes and Crocs, even in the depths of winter, and save showering and getting changed for when we get home, to minimise public showdowns.

We sit watching our girls. Clem is listening intently to the teacher. Hope and Emily are splashing water in each other's faces. It looks playful. I hope it doesn't escalate.

I'm caught off guard by this other mother talking to me, not that I'm antisocial, just that I've not chit chatted much with other parents here. We've been in the area for ten years, and it's been nearly nine years since I became a mum, but I'm still not sure where I fit. It's friendly around here. I greet most people at the school gate – there is a sense of community and comradery. But lots of people grew up in the area, with life-long friends and family a stone's throw away. It's hard to penetrate that. And it's hard to find points of connection when my experience of becoming a parent is wildly different from the norm. Sure, there are similarities, stories shared at the school gate that have me laughing along in agreement – we're all raising children, worrying about their development, rejoicing in their achievements, battling with exhaustion. It's the same... but it's not. I feel lonely in my experience; our journey has its unique challenges that I feel unable to fully express. I rarely feel able to get my head above water enough to take a look around and register everything else that's going on. And even if I do for a moment, something comes along – like *this*... I drum my fingers on my phone – leaving me frantically treading water again.

I watch Hope, while trying to systematically sort through my feelings. I'm shocked. The last time we saw Tegan – granted, it was a long time ago now – she was making concerted efforts to turn her life around. And when I periodically check her Facebook profile, as I was doing today, she's always seemed... *fine*. But now *this.* Her unexpected, unexplained death.

I have an urge to call Jo, and lament the fact that I can't. However much we've thrived without social services as the third parent in our family, I miss Jo; her calm, professional presence. She was always our first port of call in any crisis. We still keep in touch – she receives our annual elf picture at Christmas each year with delight and we meet up from time to time – but I bite my lip on bothering her with things like this, things she left behind with her retirement.

Hope's attempting to float in a star shape on her back. She keeps sinking. She's tired. My heart aches for her. She never knew Tegan. She was only ever a name. The name of the women who carried her in her tummy and birthed her. But she's significant; the first cog in Hope's story. And she's gone.

I feel a strong need to gather Hope in my arms. It's been just me and Jeremy for a long time now – the only parents they have, the ones who love them, protect them and invest in their lives. But for some reason I'm feeling it deeply right now – now Tegan's gone – I really *am* the only mum Hope has.

Never able to systematically address my feelings – unable to keep my thoughts on well-trodden tacks, however hard I try – my mind has now trespassed into territory I try to keep fenced off. I'm imagining Mum here with me – as she would be if she were alive. She'd be laughing at Hope's antics, cheering William on, and crouching down at the edge of the pool to hear what Emily wants to whisper in her ear. She'd say, "I wouldn't change their fun-loving spirits for compliance, even for a second!" and I'd laugh and say, "It's exhausting but I agree, they're spirited, and I *love* it." She'd have noticed my expression change when I looked at my phone, asked me what's wrong, and we'd have talked about Tegan, and Hope, and why social services didn't call to tell us this phenomenally important piece of information. And I'd have sorted my head out.

She'd have asked about Bill and Pat, and how Jeremy is coping with his dad's deterioration and whether Pat's had the results of her scan. I would have told her about my period being late this month and how I can't help but always wonder, and hope, like it's an uncontrollable impulse, despite being in the throes of perimenopause. We'd have put my small world to rights, right here beside the pool, with all this chaos going on around us. She'd be sat here now with her arm around me. A constant, reassuring presence.

But she's not.

I try to think of something else. I'm not remotely in control of my feelings right now. Grief is sneaky. It makes me nervous; catching me up when I least expect. Making me choke. I'm forty-six next month, but I still need my mum. She's been dead eleven years but I'm still liable to cry right here in the middle of my kids' swimming lesson – my sobs absorbed by the echoes of voices and splashing, my tears lost on the wet floor.

"Oh my God!" Clem's mum – I never asked her name, we're defined by our children – exclaims, making me jump again. "Look what she's wearing!" She shows me her phone. I think it's Kim Kardashian, but I can't say for sure. I couldn't care less right now, and I've got zero chat.

"*Hideous*!" I say this more forcefully than I'd planned and then immediately wonder if I said the right thing. Maybe I misjudged her tone and she really *likes* what she's wearing. I avoid eye contact and organise the kids' bathrobes in a little pile next to me. Hopefully she's picking up on the fact that I don't want to talk.

I stew until the end of the lesson, my thoughts circling while I watch William steadily losing focus and peeling away from the group, doing his own thing by the side of the pool. I feel proud of him. It's a lot – a stimulating day at school followed by a tiring thirty-minute swimming lesson.

There has been a national shortage of his ADHD medication recently; he's on a third of the dose he should be on, and he feels it in his mind and in his body. We weren't sure about medication initially, worried it could change his personality in some way, but the nurse explained how it helps to slow his brain down, giving him more control over his reactions and impulses. He's still as William as ever on the medication, just less overwhelmed.

As soon as he's out of the pool, he grabs his towel and says he's going to the loo. He may well need a wee, but I have a sense that he's just needing to escape somewhere quiet for a moment. Away from the constant, indiscriminate noise and bright lights. He pauses, asking if I'm ok, clearly sensing I'm not. My heart swells at his gentleness and sensitivity.

Emily shakes herself off like a dog and comes and perches on my knee, wriggling around unable to keep still, her bony wet bottom leaving a wet patch on my skirt. "Great swimming, Emily lady," I whisper. It's really clicked recently – she still needs a float most of the time, but can manage a few strokes on her own. I've relished the satisfaction she's felt.

She started school a few months ago, confronted daily by new experiences, but seems to be taking it all in her stride.

She finds it hard to concentrate and sit still for hours on end, but she enjoys it, which is far more important to me than her academic achievement at the age of four.

She looks at me, grinning and wrinkling her nose, slipping off my knee and rummaging in my bag, asking for a snack. Sometimes I wish we could linger in a moment a while longer before having to talk about snacks.

I help Hope remove her goggles, holding her glasses ready while using the other hand to protect my bag from scavengers.

"Did you know I have a *magic* POWER?!" Hope asks, steadying her glasses on her nose while she pulls her Minion bathrobe over her head.

"Shhh, do you have to speak so loudly Hopeful?!" I shield an ear with my free hand – the other still occupied protecting my bag from potential snack thieves. Hope has one volume. She's about half a metre from my head but is shouting. It's doing nothing for my headache. "Tell me about your magic power?" I say, changing my tone.

She comes close to my ear and whispers, "I can speak *Minion*." I pull her close and give her a little squeeze. She smells of chlorine.

"Nooooo! Really? That's a cool power, Hopeful!" One glance at her face confirms to me that she actually thinks she can. When do we lose this unimpeded belief in ourselves? I hope she can speak Minion forever.

We make our way to the car, scooping William up on the way. None of my three seem able to move in a straight line, ricocheting off walls and climbing on benches, their bathrobes streaming behind them like capes. There are steps down to the carpark, but who needs steps when you can slide down the railings or walk through the flowerbeds? "Avoid the flowers please, Emily!" I might as well be talking to myself. She continues as if she hasn't heard me. Sometimes I wonder whether I actually said the thing out loud, or whether no one can hear the frequency of my voice.

We blare Taylor Swift in the car on the way home. William is pretending to be annoyed with the choice of music, but is secretly loving it. I sing along too, feeling a weight lift as I sing 'Shake it off' at the top of my lungs. I only have to pull over and stop the car once to get everyone to, "stop throwing things at each other or I might crash!" during the seventeen-minute drive home, which isn't bad considering the wild state everyone's in.

"Is Grandad Bill going to die like Chilli did?" Hope asks loudly as she gets out of the car.

I don't know where this has come from. It seems out of the blue, though I guess she must have been thinking about it since our conversation about Grandad's health yesterday. Chilli, her beloved cat, was hit by a car a few weeks ago. It was traumatic when our neighbour brought her round, Hope's first experience of loss. Now loss feels real to her. Things die. And now Grandad's ill.

I remind her that Grandad isn't afraid of dying; that he believes there is a beautiful place beyond this world where he will be close to God, close enough to walk with him. "He's full of hope."

"Like me," she adds. "And he's funny like me."

"Yes," I laugh, enjoying how she seamlessly links death, hope and humour in her mind. I hope she continues to adopt some of Bill's cheerful approach to life; he even managed to remain light-hearted when his hospital bed was delivered by the hospice last week, trying out all the 'knobs' with glee and searching for the 'ejector' button.

I wonder how and when we'll be able to tell Hope about Tegan, and how it might make her feel. Possibly not much, initially – it won't affect her day-to-day life as it would to lose Grandad – but I wonder if her death could feel more complex for Hope in time. This journey will never be simple. If I'm honest I feel overwhelmed by it most of the time. We have no plan, other than to love as completely, as carefully and as intentionally as we know how; lovingly muddling through.

Jeremy's ready to receive us as we walk through the door, providing the energy I lack. He gives me a quick kiss, then pauses, searching my face. "I'll tell you later," I say, immediately feeling lighter at the prospect of sharing the weight of the latest loss. Together we usher the kids in the direction of the bathroom, raising our voices over the din, simultaneously revelling in and agonising over the constant joy and strain of life with these three.

I'm holding my purple number ten bowling ball tensely; my fingers in the holes, awaiting my turn. I'm losing, but for once I don't care. I'm too preoccupied with watching the two of them. They're moving around each other carefully, with shy glances and furtive smiles. Do they look alike? They have the same wide smile, the same facial shape, the same glint in their eyes.

Maggie helps Hope position her ball on the ramp, aiming for a strike. The ball flattens all the pins bar one and Hope jumps up and down, squealing with delight, her high ponytail swinging, her glasses slipping down her nose. Maggie offers her a high five, which Hope accepts before running back to me, as if to touch base.

I catch Maggie's eye and she smiles. "Thanks for this," she says, coming alongside me. "I never thought I'd see her again. I can't quite believe it, y'know." She pauses, watching Hope as she searches for the heaviest ball she can pick up. "She looks like Tegan at that age..."

Last week, social services put me in touch with Maggie, Tegan's mum. It turns out that they'd known about Tegan's death all along, Maggie having called them on multiple occasions, asking if they could pass the message on to Hope and her brother's adoptive parents. But they never got in touch. I was mad on principle. They should have told us; I shouldn't have found out on social media.

But they did give me Maggie's number, and we met for coffee last week, equally nervous and curious. I couldn't help turning over the things I'd read about Tegan's past in her file all those years ago – the instability and seeming neglect of her upbringing. Who was the woman in the background? The woman who shaped Tegan. Would she be the monster I'd imagined?

Far from it. Maggie was tentative, but warm, and we connected as mothers. I understood that she did the best she could in hard circumstances. "We'd just started to patch up our relationship when she died..." Maggie had told me, utterly dejected by the timing of Tegan's death. We talked about it a bit – her death – how she was found dead in her bed. People assumed she'd accidently overdosed, but not enough drugs were found in her system. The postmortem was inconclusive; those close to Tegan left forever living in the unknown. But aside from mothering and death, we mainly talked about Hope. Beautiful, spirited, Minion-loving, hope-filled Hope.

She wanted to meet her.

So here we are, living another surreal life-moment, rolling bowling balls with the woman who birthed the woman who birthed Hope.

When Jeremy and I found the right moment to tell Hope that her birth mother had died, she'd shrugged and said, "Oh, that's ok. You're my mum so it doesn't matter." And that was that. The hard conversation we'd been putting off, done in seconds. But she was curious when I told her about Maggie. William had a birth sister, and Emily a birth half-sister in Sienna, something Hope was envious of. The prospect of a birth grandmother sounded interesting. And we wanted to encourage that instinct. Birth families shouldn't be feared.

The game ends appropriately with Hope winning, and once she's finished celebrating – punching the air – Maggie asks, falteringly, if she can give her a hug. Hope nods and they hug, lightly; as if Hope is still a little unsure, cautiously warming to her, and as if Maggie is allowing Hope the freedom to peel away when she needs to.

And as we walk towards the exit Maggie says to me again, "she does look so like Tegan..." then adds, pointedly, "but she's *your* daughter, Clare."

EPILOGUE

Jeremy

This view is becoming familiar. The expansive, mosaic stone wall, angular arch, blue curtains and coffin centre stage. I was sitting in this pew on the front row just two months ago. Dad had, "gone for a party in heaven," as Hope had put it.
The winter morning light had forced its way past the cloud cover, welcomed in through the vast ceiling-high windows to the right.

We're bathed in soft light again today, in this cathedral-like building; cavernous and majestic. I'm in turmoil, but the air in the space around me is still. I want this peace to seep in and claim me.

The last time I was here I was sitting next to Mum. I'd reached out for her hand when their wonderful minister, Sam Griffiths, committed Dad's body – 'Ashes to ashes, dust to dust' – clutching it and looking straight ahead but not at anything in particular. It had felt like holding the dead bird Emily found a few days before; soft, silky, a cluster of tiny bones that could break if I held too tight. So I held her hand lightly, as she sat perfectly still.

People keep saying that she died because she couldn't bear living without Dad. But they're wrong; she was heartbroken, but she wanted to live. She had plans for her garden, where she would plant spring bulbs and play with her grandchildren. She didn't give up; the cancer claimed her. We shouldn't be here saying goodbye to her, not yet, and not so soon after losing Dad.

William, Hope and Emily made her 'get well soon' cards, even when her prognosis was terminal. She had loved them, propping them up next to her bedside, and I'd fed off their hope and confidence that somehow everything would be alright, willing myself to adopt their bright child-like perspective. Their cards are in the coffin with Mum now, tucked between her bird-like hands and chest.

I find myself thinking back to Clare's mum's funeral, twelve years ago, and I think of the scan pictures we'd placed in the coffin with her. It had been so dark in that crematorium; we had been stifled and enclosed, surrounded by dusty air, heavy with loss heaped on loss. But right now the space around us is bright and open, hinting to my distressed soul that there is more, and reminding me of how far we've come and how much has changed for good.

We will always live with loss – it underscores everything at the moment – but life is no longer defined by it. Life is full, dynamic and bright. William, Hope and Emily are the embodiment of our hope; it is no longer thin and unfocused. They are vibrant and fun; dramatic and complex. They replenish us and consume us; sustain us and drain us.

They'll be in their first lesson at school now: Hope sitting at the front, her hand enthusiastically in the air; Emily wriggling around, her beautiful mind noticing every movement; William telling Mrs Everett something, with her leaning in wide-eyed and attentive. I find myself making a mental note to tell Mum how much William's confidence has grown recently, before realising that I can't.

The regal roar of the organ summons me to my feet and back to reality, where hope meets loss in a perpetual dance. Rachel's David hits the keys on the organ and the intimate cluster of family around me begin to sing, ‘Love divine, all loves excelling.’ I sing in a whisper, grateful for the organ providing the gusto I lack, allowing the words to move through me; singing of being lost, not in our ‘troubled’, ‘trembling’ hearts, but in ‘wonder, love and praise’.

We file out, a cold February breeze licking our tear-stained faces; words of hope resounding in our ears. It’s quiet, apart from the birdsong, and as I put one foot in front of the other, the rhythmic crunch of the gravel under my feet, I feel a deep peace claim me. I’m surprised by it. It surpasses understanding. I know it’s not from within me, and I can only believe it’s God’s spirit, sustaining me and giving me the strength and conviction to know that however hard it is – this journey we’re on – it will be ok. We are weathered, yet somehow stronger; our faith simpler, yet deeper. And as we step into this new season, whatever it holds, I can’t help but wonder, how hard can it be?

## Acknowledgements

Baby J: We hit the jackpot when we got you as our social worker! Without you we wouldn't be the family we are today. We absolutely love you J and we're grateful for all you did for our children (and us!).

Karen & Ruthie: You've lived these chapters with us for real and you know the ones we've left unsaid... Thank you for being a part of our lives from the very beginning. Life is richer for your friendship. Let's climb Kilimanjaro!

Jane: A random interview took us on a crazy writing journey together but we've loved it. Thank you for taking a risk and saying yes. Thank you for immersing yourself in our past and present. We hope our friendship will grow into the future! You are an incredible woman who's skilled at taking our ramblings and crafting something beautiful.

Lauren Osborne for your incredible blackwork illustrations & **Matt from Olio Creative** for designing our cover!

John & Penny, Pam & Stephen, Juliet, Liz, Mike, Claire & Jeremy (the other ones!) Cat, Graham & Jackie, Audrey, Busy, Jeremy (the other one), Joan, Jessica, Marcus, Robert, Tony, Jan & Ken, Phillipa & Grant, Ian, Gina. You've all been a part of our lives at different points and haven't left! We are SO grateful for your wisdom, your prayers, your encouragement and for being there in the good and the bad times!

Liz, Ellie, Claire, Amy, Kymberly, Bethan, Luke, George, Martha, Bethany, Sammi, Julie, Caroline, Debbie, Kerry, Chrissie, Becs, Charlotte, Diane. The school run wouldn't be the same without you. We are grateful for caring about us as a family, for asking how we're doing, and for teaching our children!

Carol, Rachel, David, James, Sam, Martha, Isaac, Nancy, Ross, Beth, Mike, Shirley, Jean & John, Anne & Ray, Caroline & Ant, Jess, Laura, Miranda, Margaret & Tony, Mark & Tony, Joanne – thank you for your love, prayers, encouragement and walking this life with us.

Paul & Linda, Lynn, Helen, Gareth, Vicky: Thank you for taking a risk all those years ago and sharing our story. We're grateful you became a part of our lives and have loved and prayed for us and our children.

To the birth parents: We recognise that your loss has been our gain.

The children wanted to thank their teachers, Vicky the hairdresser, the Minions, Taylor Swift and the cats.

Jeremy: Without you there'd be no us! We've made it through sleepless nights together. We've faced heartache together. We've faced doubts and fears together. We've laughed... We've cried... We've dreamed... We've wondered how hard can it be...? There's no one I would rather do life with than you. I love you!!!! Here's to the easy teenage years... together!

Clare: I couldn't have done it without you! Through thick and thin you have been there supporting me. We became a great team able to overcome everything life (and social services) has thrown at us. We've laughed, cried and celebrated together and I'd not have wanted to do any of those with anyone else.

William, Hope and Emily: Becoming your parents has been our greatest joy. We haven't always got it right – we're learning on the job. But we're looking forward to see you grow up and see your dreams become a reality. From meeting Taylor Swift, to playing Minecraft with Preston to changing the world you live in because of who you are. We believe in you! We love you more than we'll ever be able to tell you – lets go have a lifetime of adventure together!

Printed in Dunstable, United Kingdom

65090436R00137